The Art
of
Coloring War

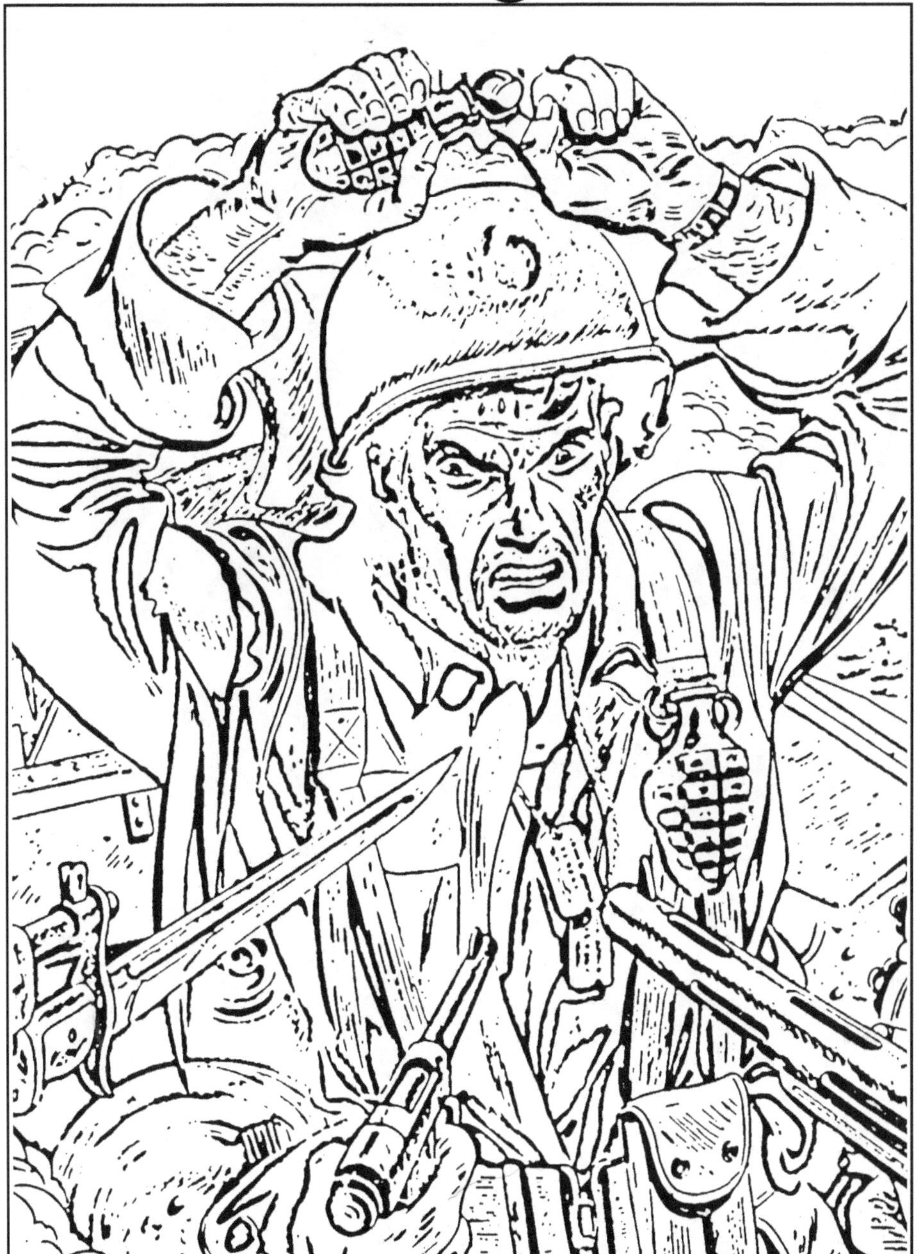

The Art of Coloring War

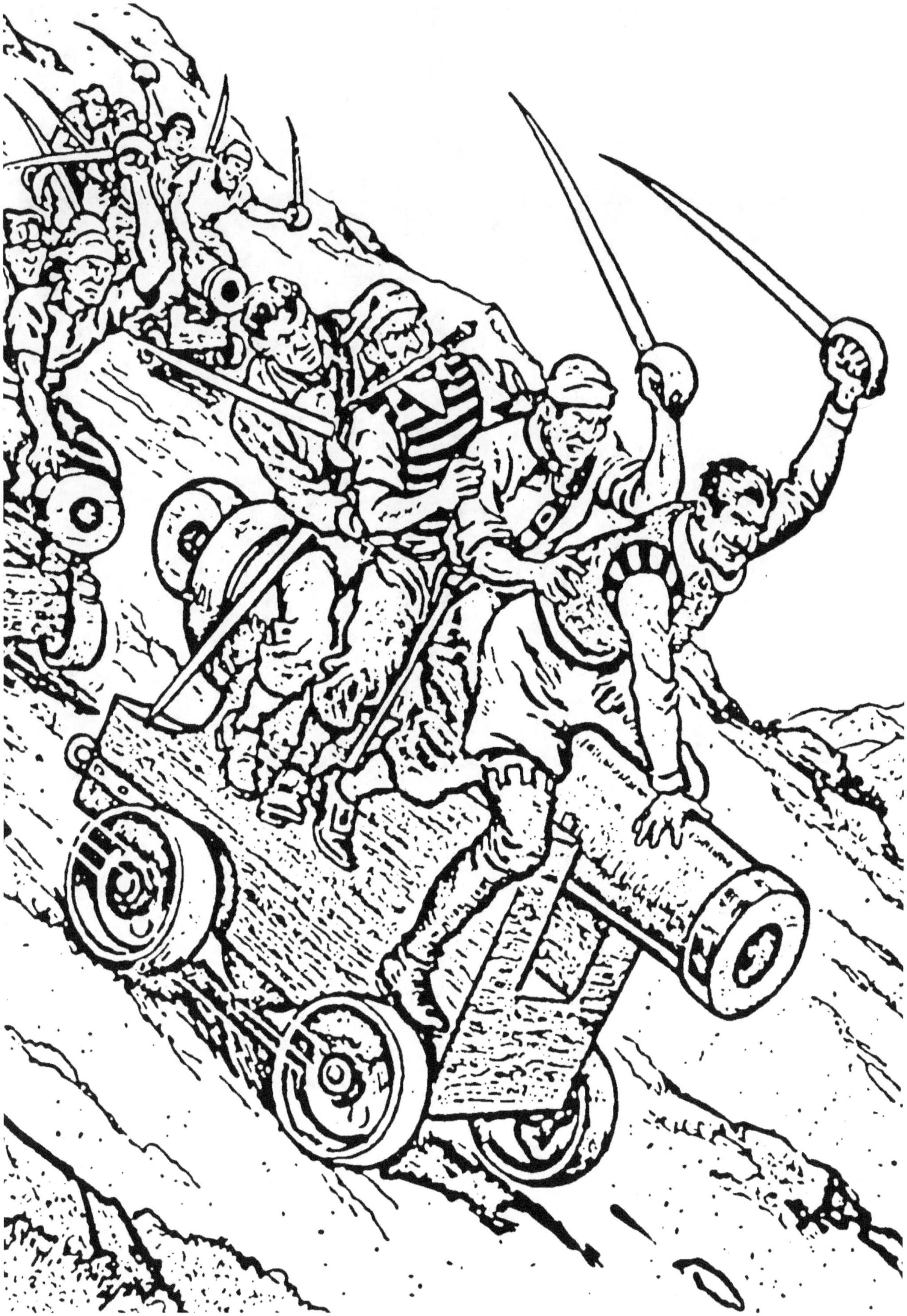

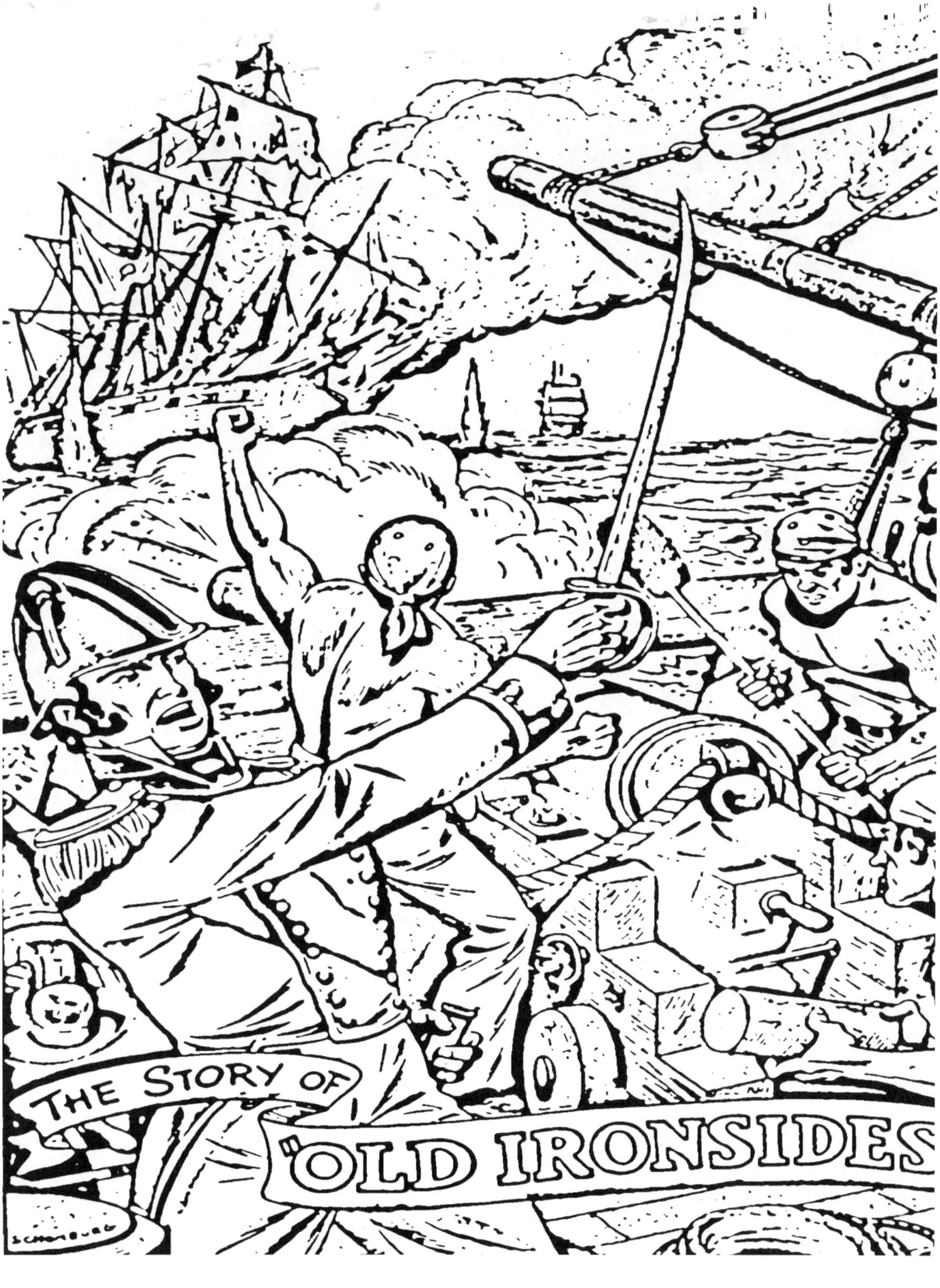
THE STORY OF
"OLD IRONSIDES"
SCHOMBURG

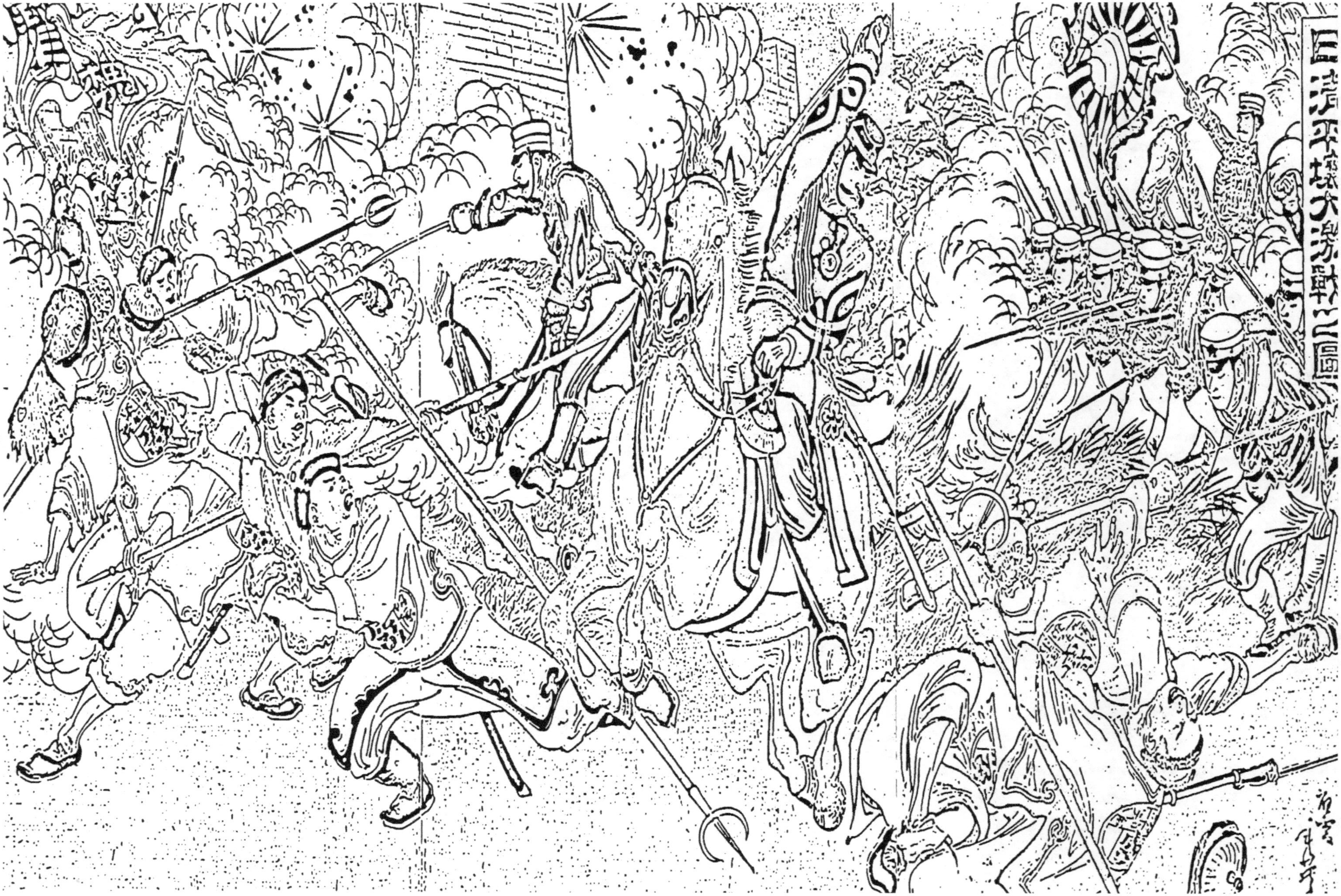
日清平壌大激戦之圖

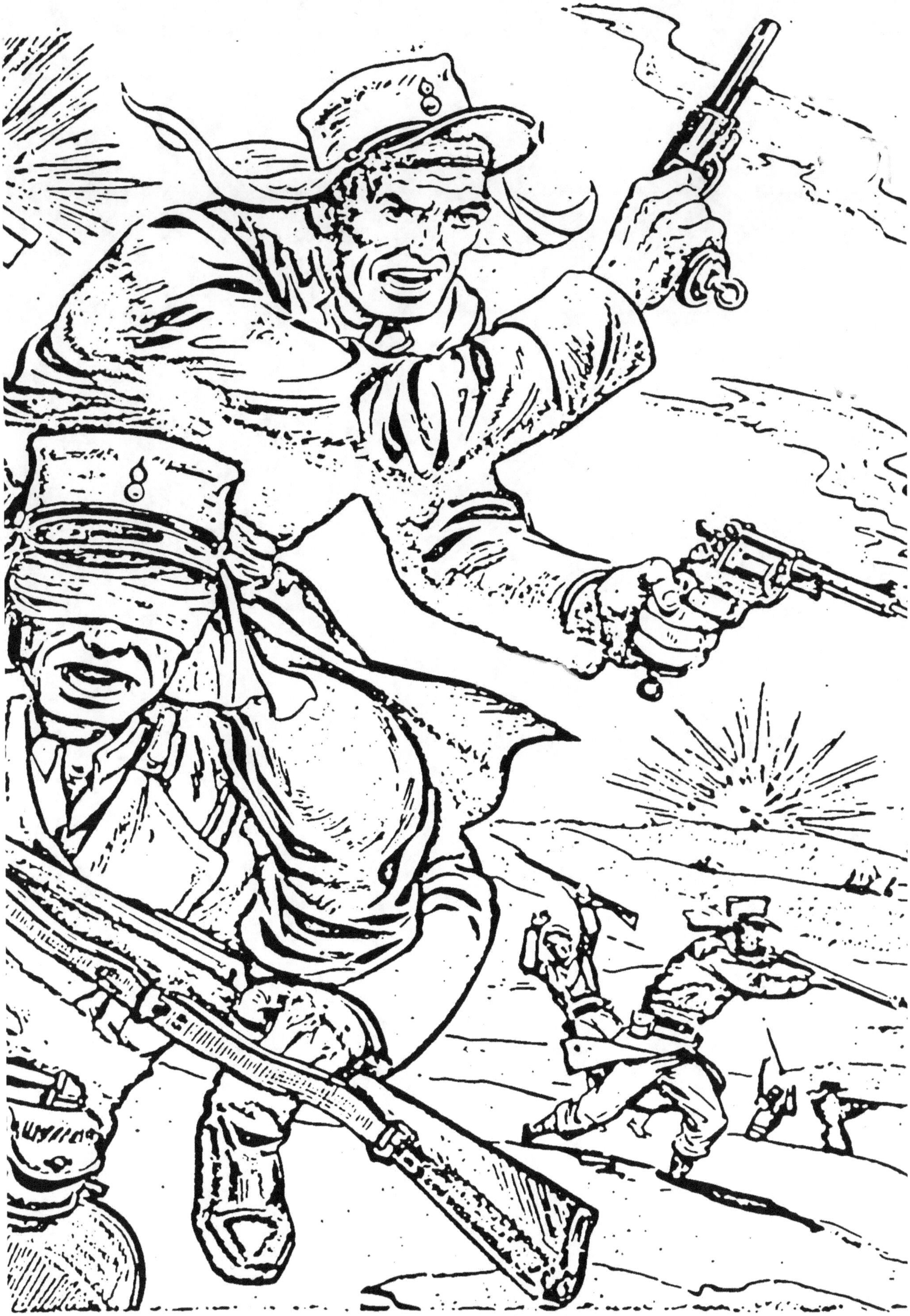

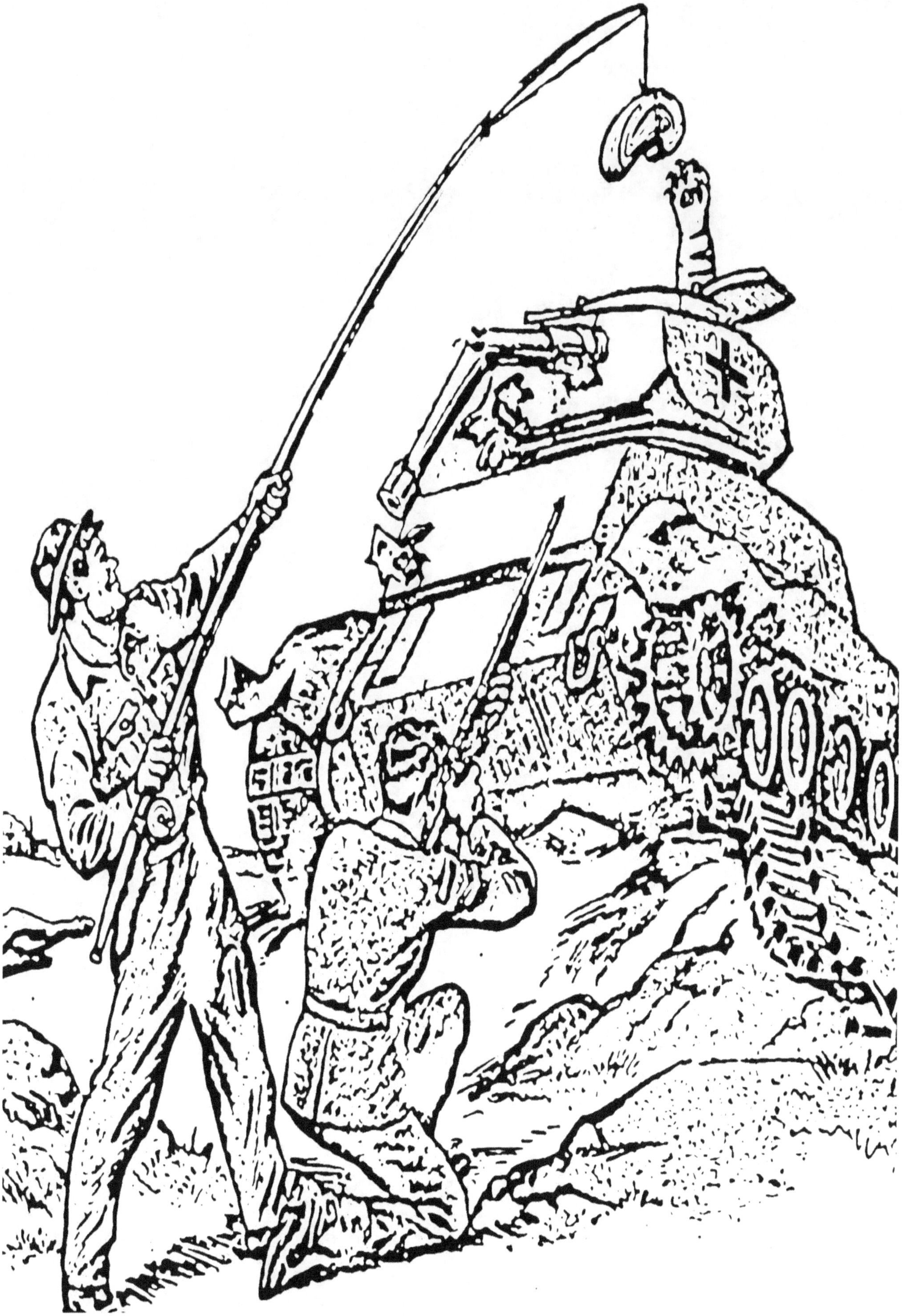

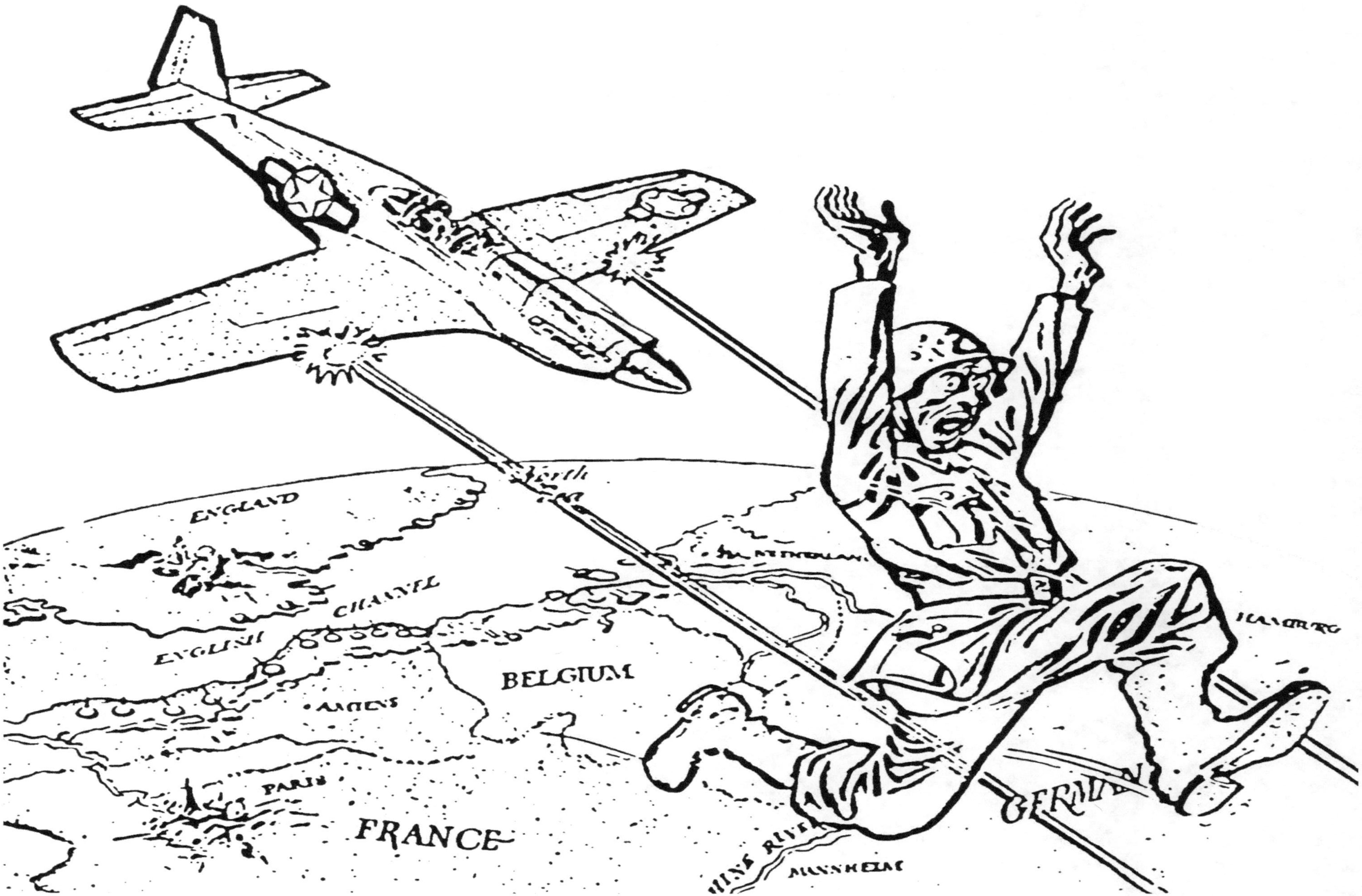
ENGLAND
CHANNEL
BELGIUM
PARIS
FRANCE

JULY
No. 3
10¢

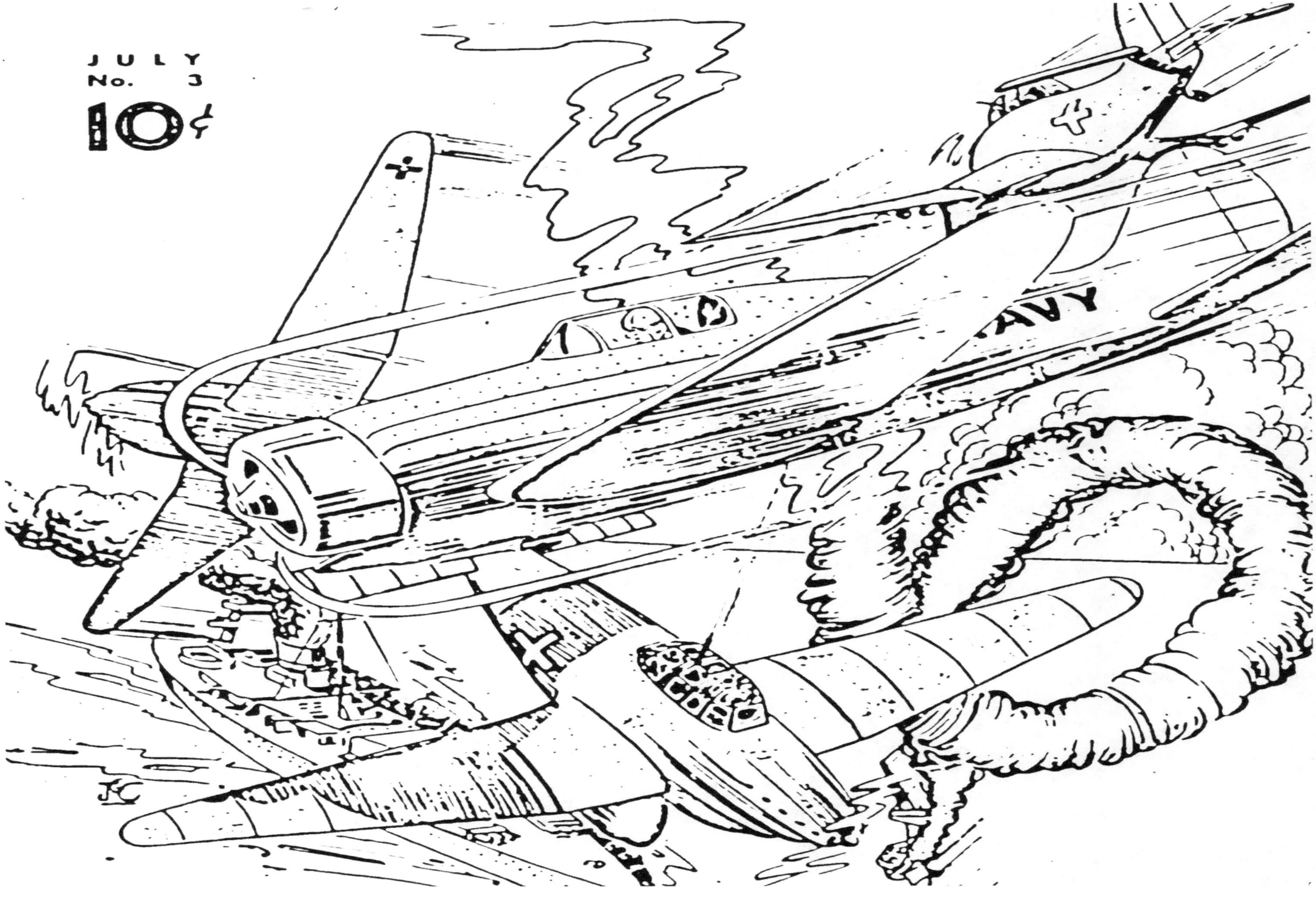

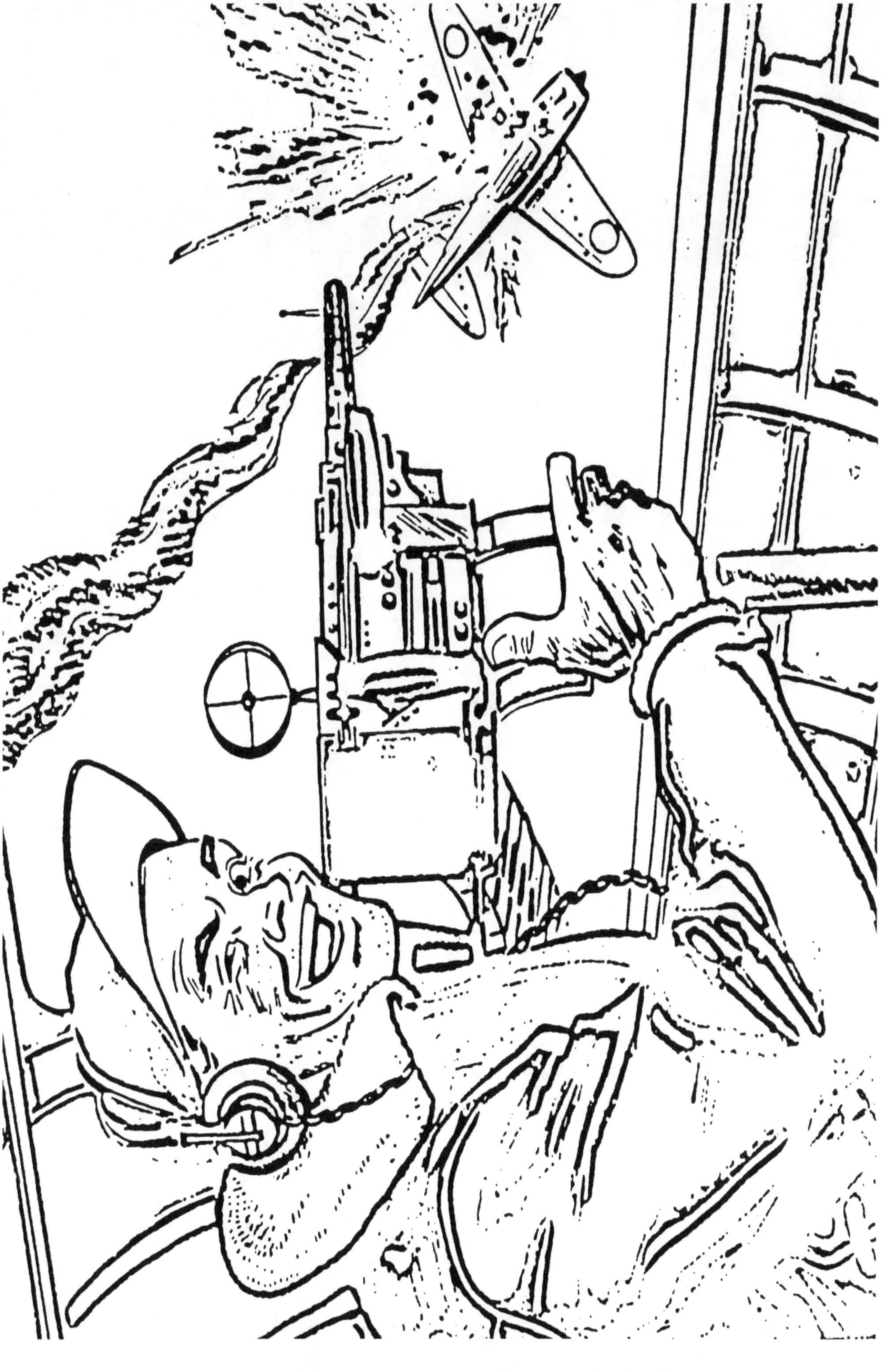

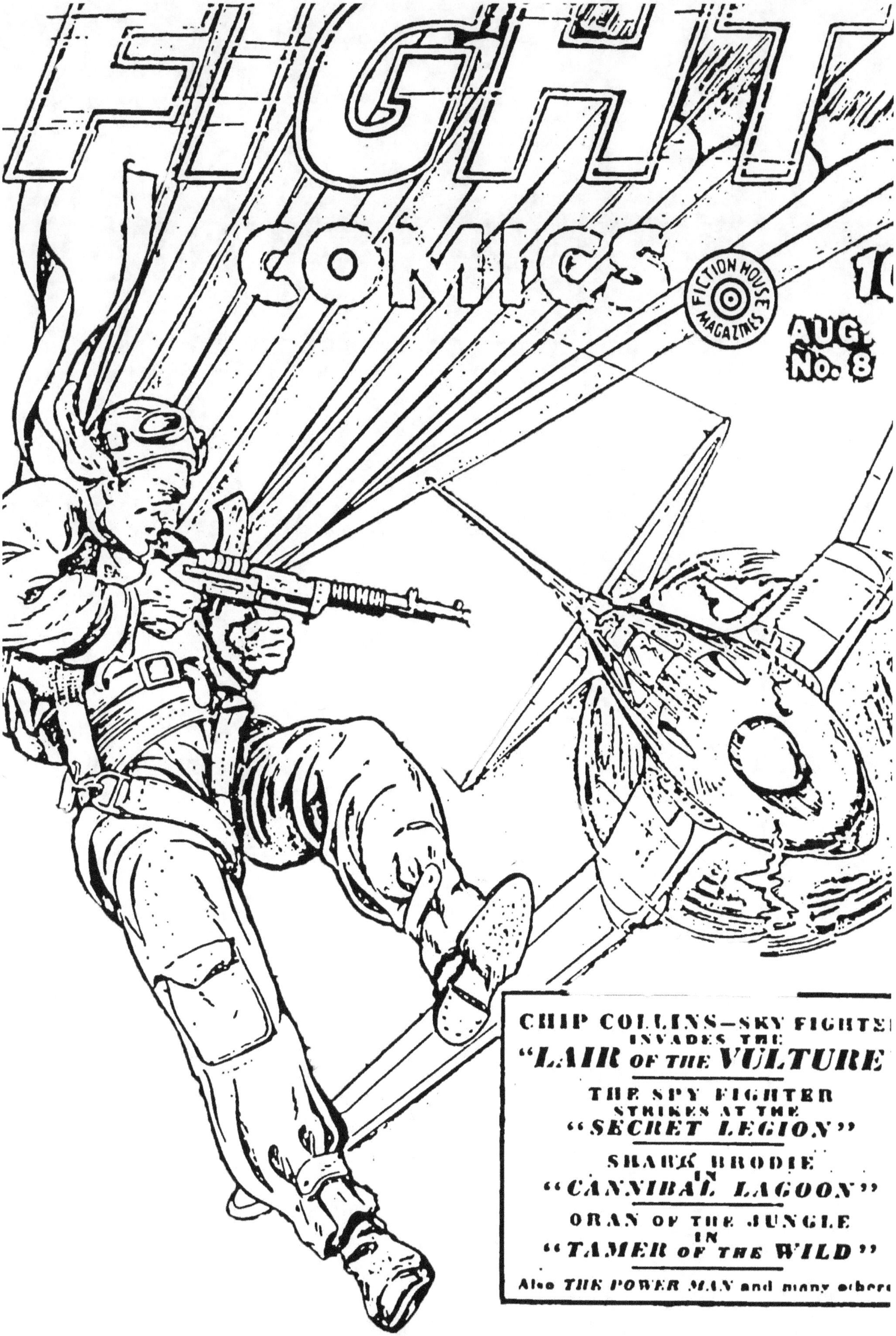

FIGHT
COMICS
FICTION HOUSE MAGAZINES
10
AUG.
No. 8
CHIP COLLINS—SKY FIGHTE
INVADES THE
"LAIR OF THE VULTURE
THE SPY FIGHTER
STRIKES AT THE
"SECRET LEGION"
SHARK BRODIE
IN
"CANNIBAL LAGOON"
ORAN OF THE JUNGLE
IN
"TAMER OF THE WILD"
Also THE POWER MAN and many other

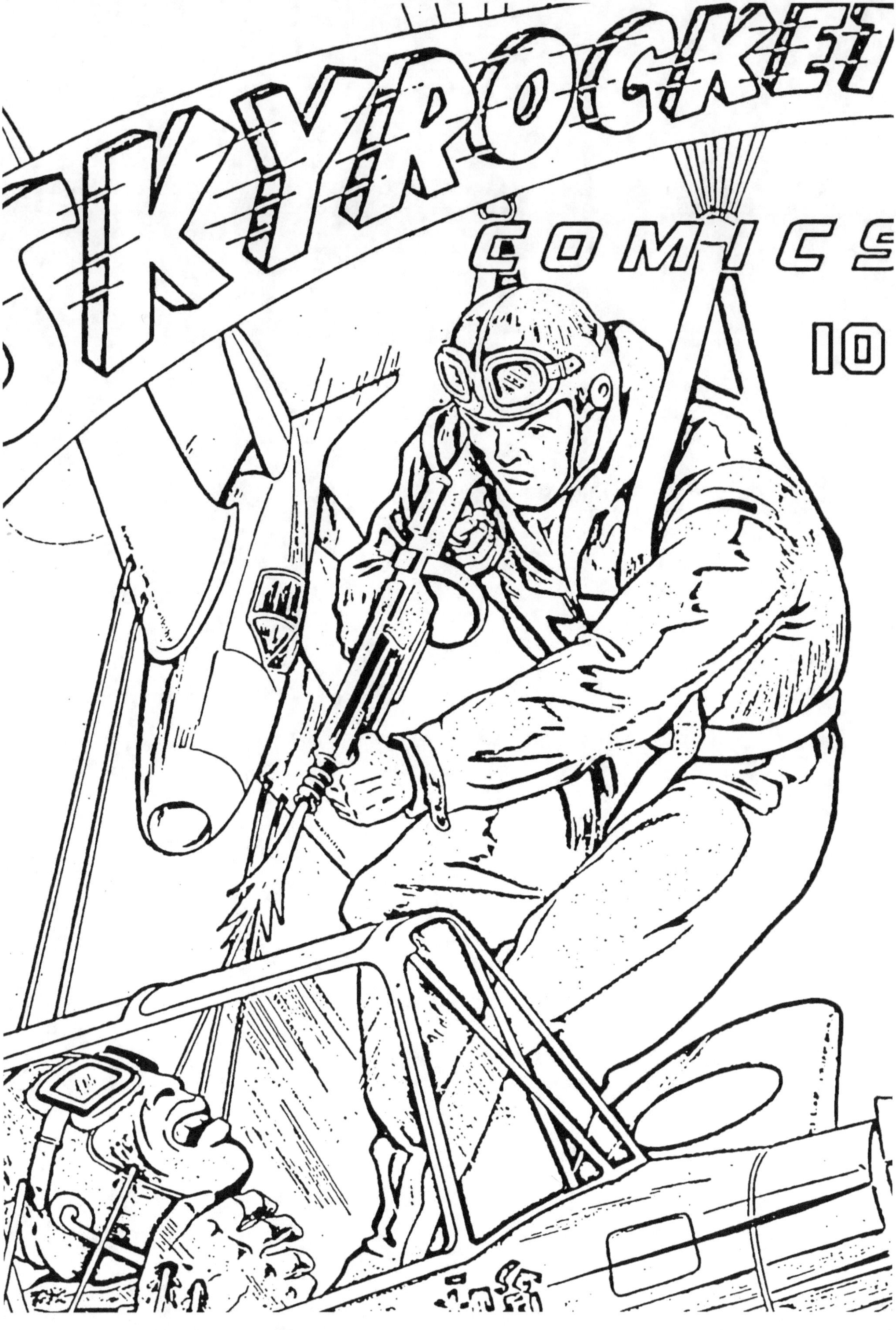
SKYROCKET
COMICS
10

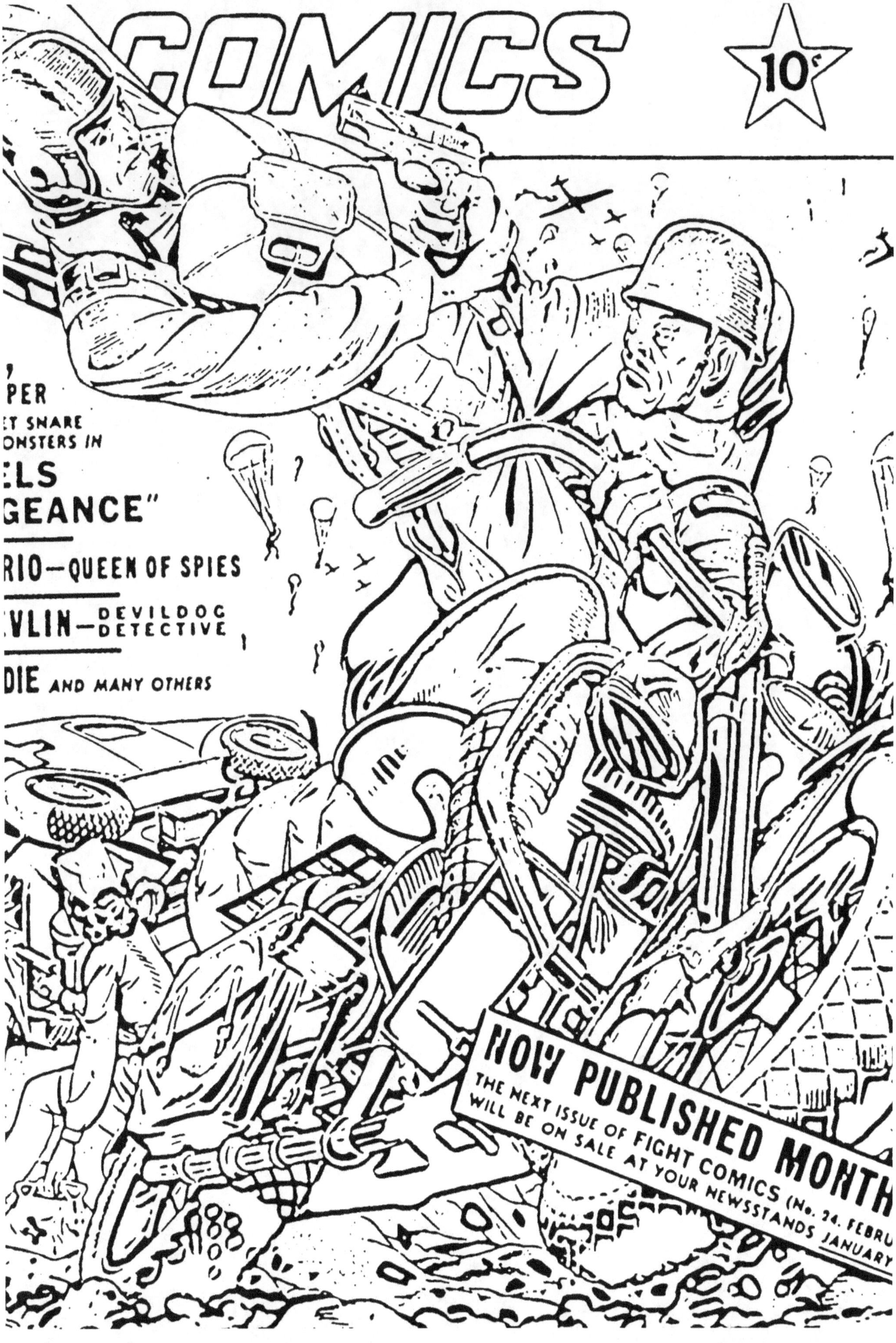
COMICS
10¢
PER
ET SNARE
ONSTERS IN
ELS
GEANCE"
RIO—QUEEN OF SPIES
VLIN—DEVILDOG DETECTIVE
DIE AND MANY OTHERS
NOW PUBLISHED MONTH
THE NEXT ISSUE OF FIGHT COMICS (No. 24, FEBRU
WILL BE ON SALE AT YOUR NEWSSTANDS JANUARY

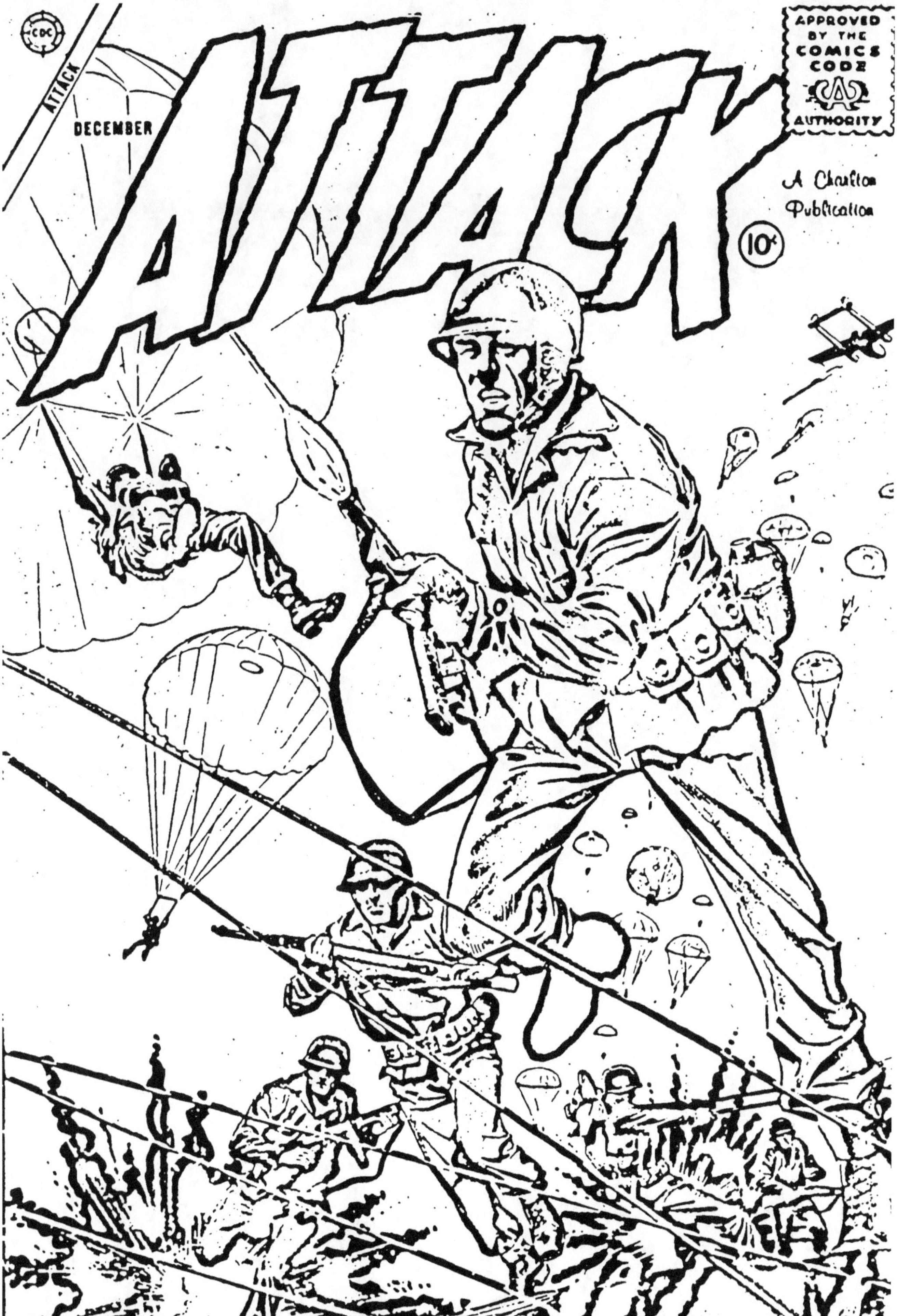
ATTACK
DECEMBER
ATTACK
APPROVED BY THE COMICS CODE AUTHORITY
A Charlton Publication
10¢

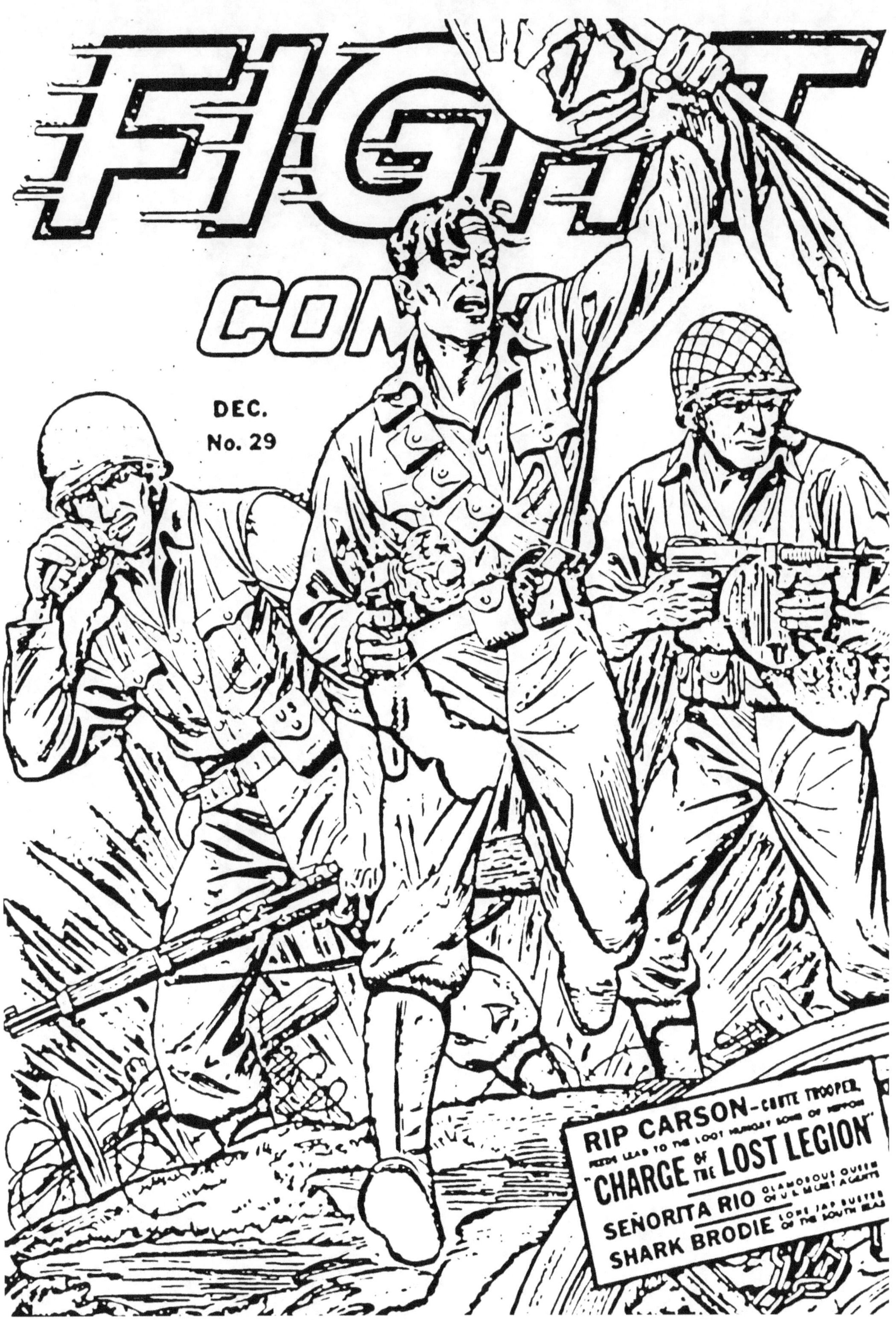
FIGHT
DEC.
No. 29
RIP CARSON
CHARGE OF THE LOST LEGION
SEÑORITA RIO
SHARK BRODIE

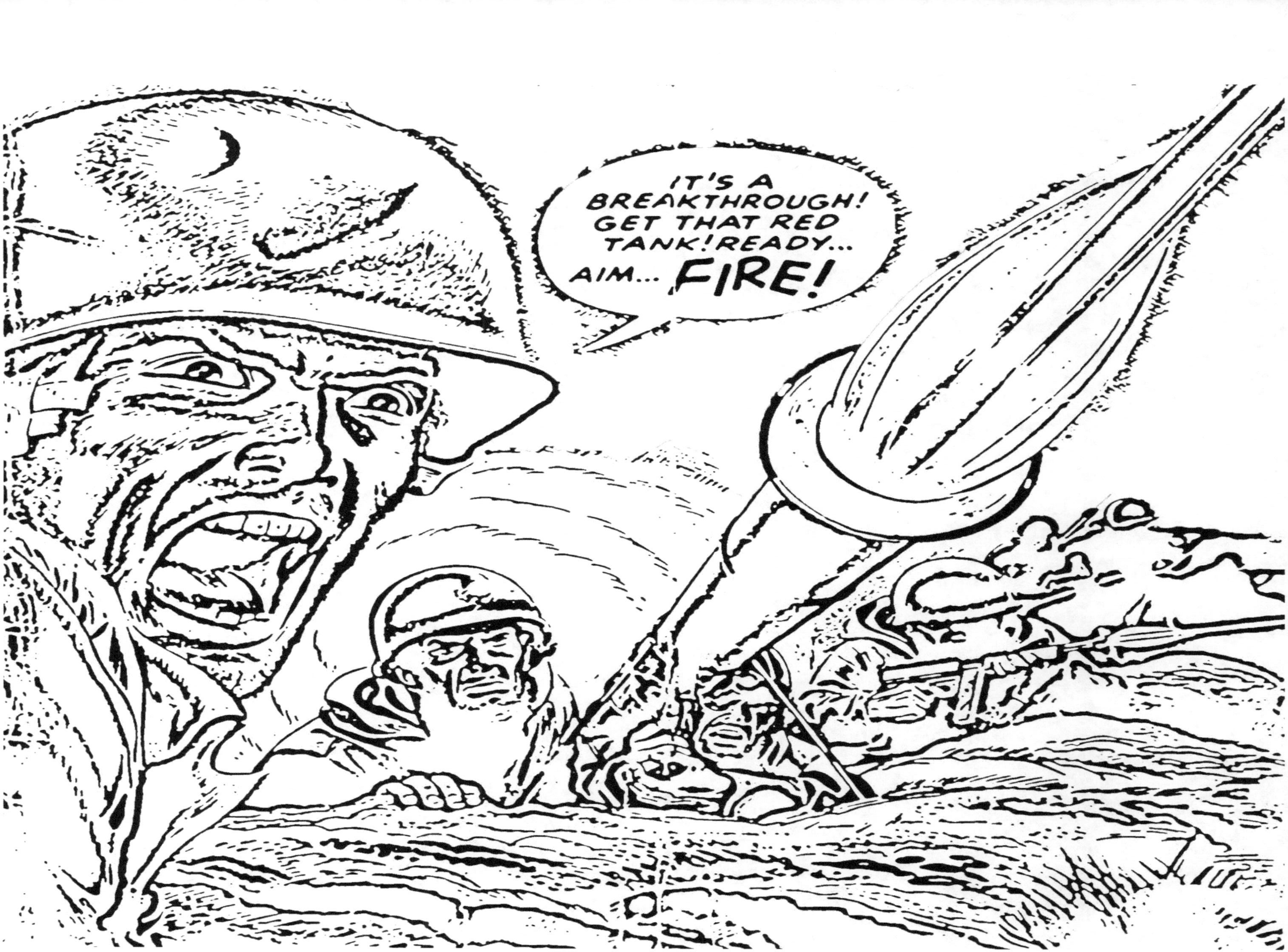
IT'S A BREAKTHROUGH! GET THAT RED TANK! READY... AIM... FIRE!

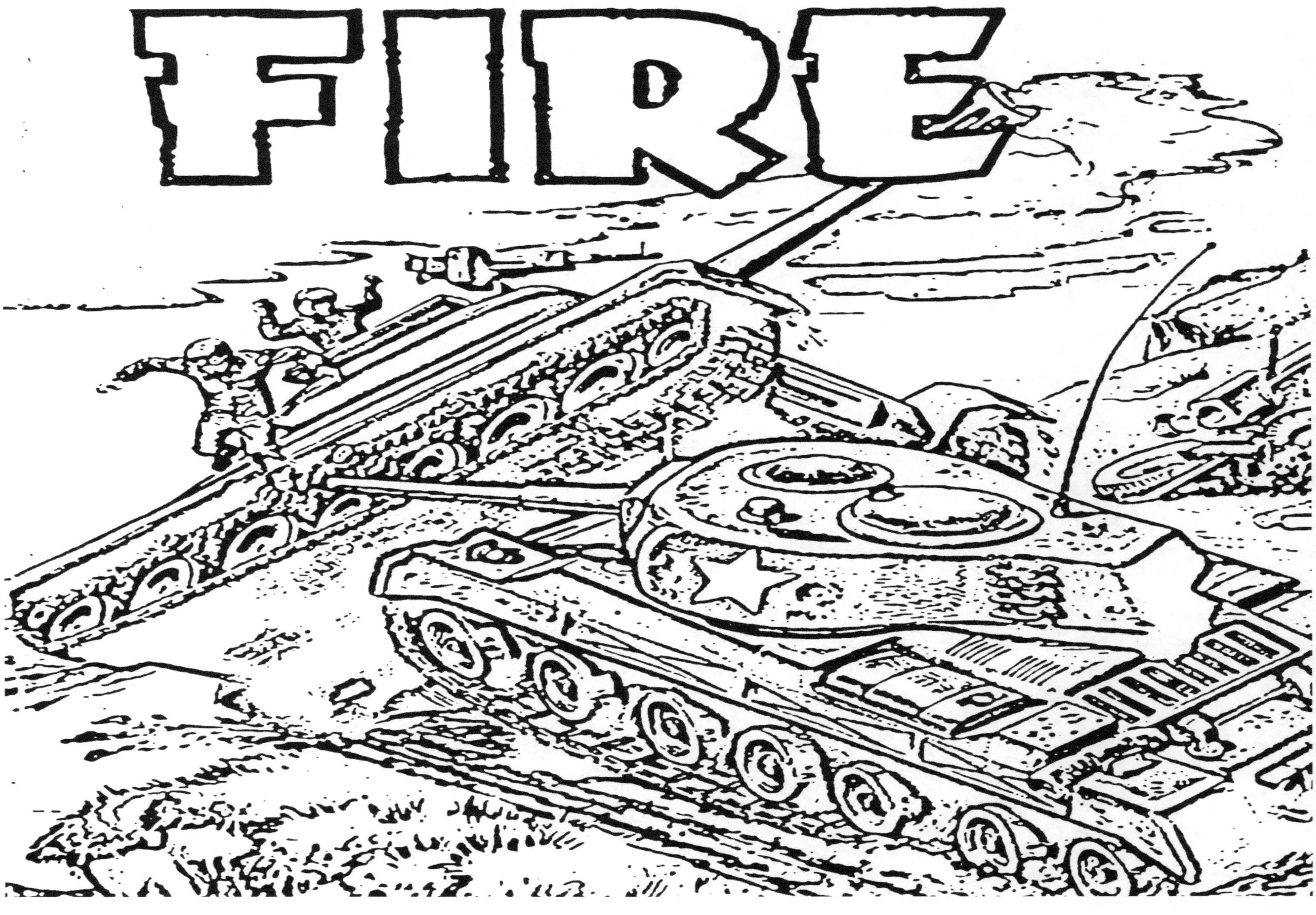
FIRE

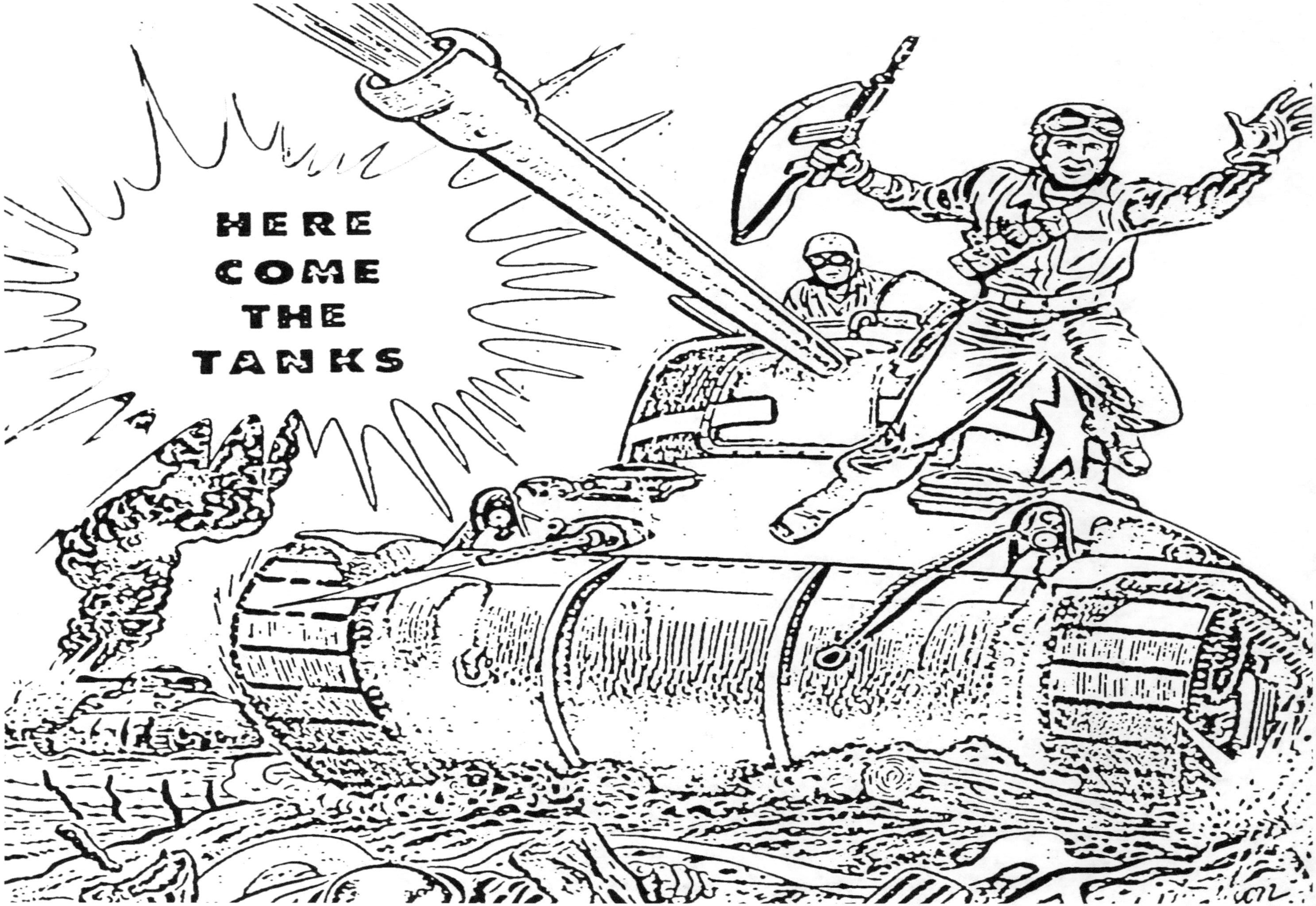
HERE COME THE TANKS

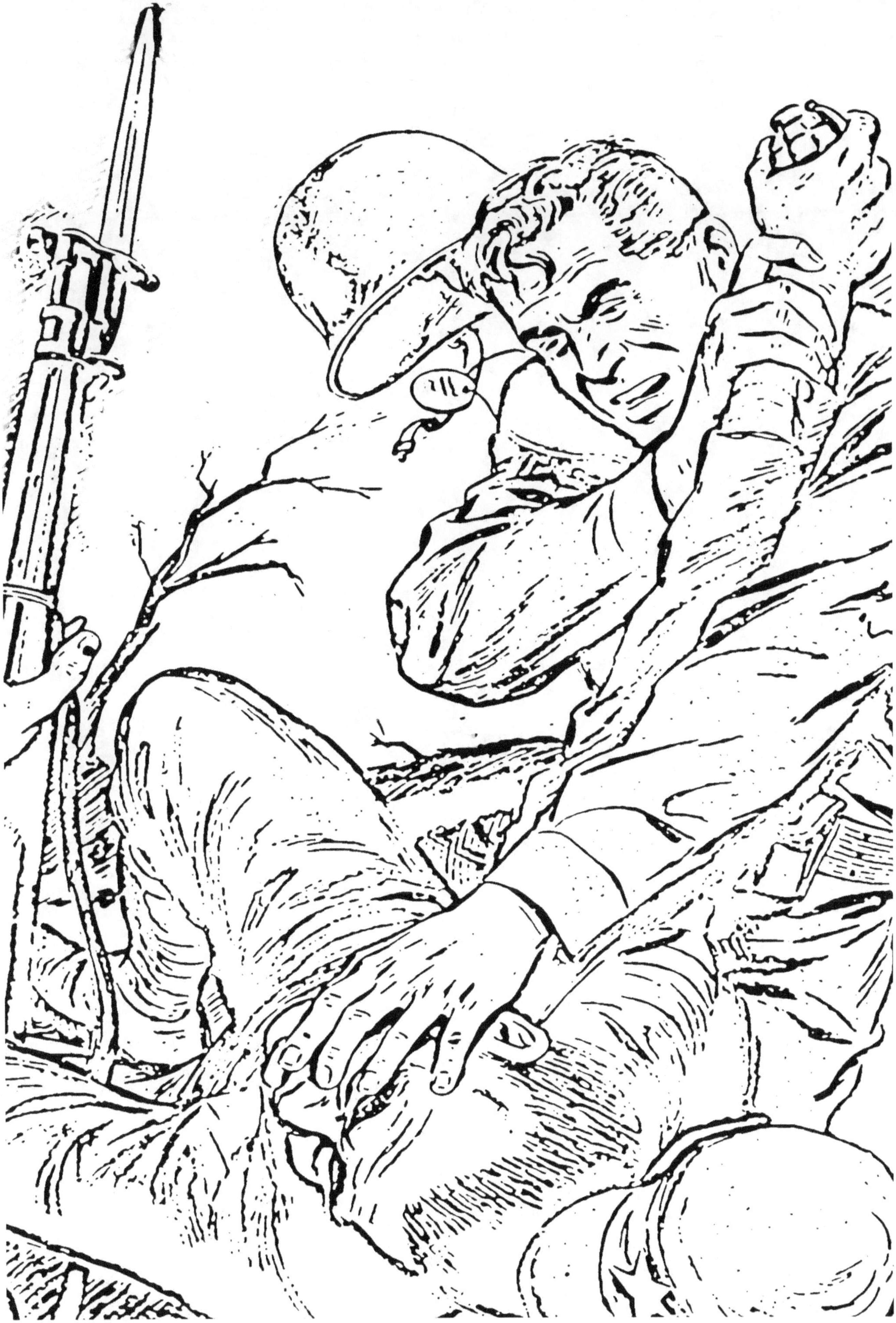

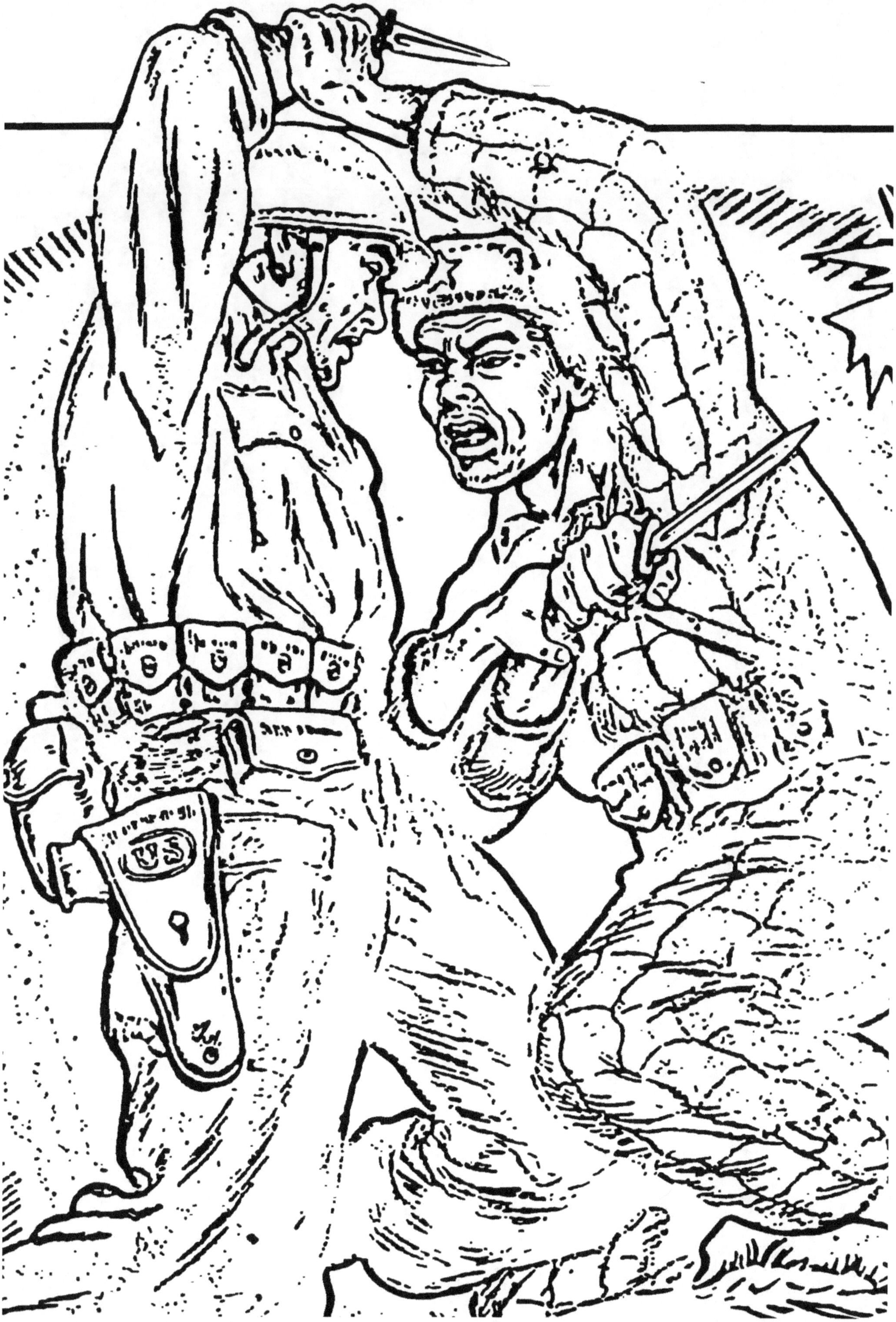

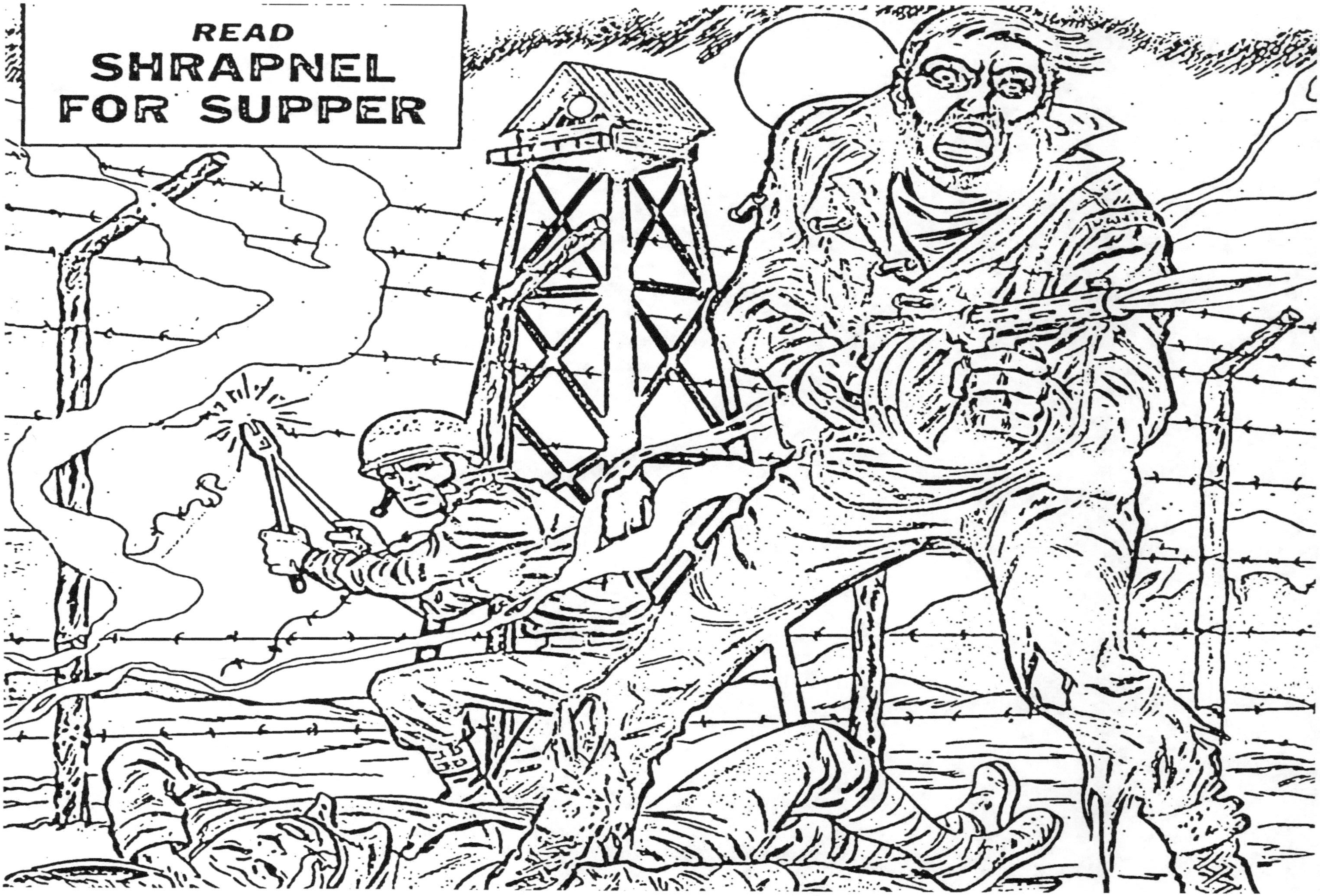
READ
SHRAPNEL
FOR SUPPER

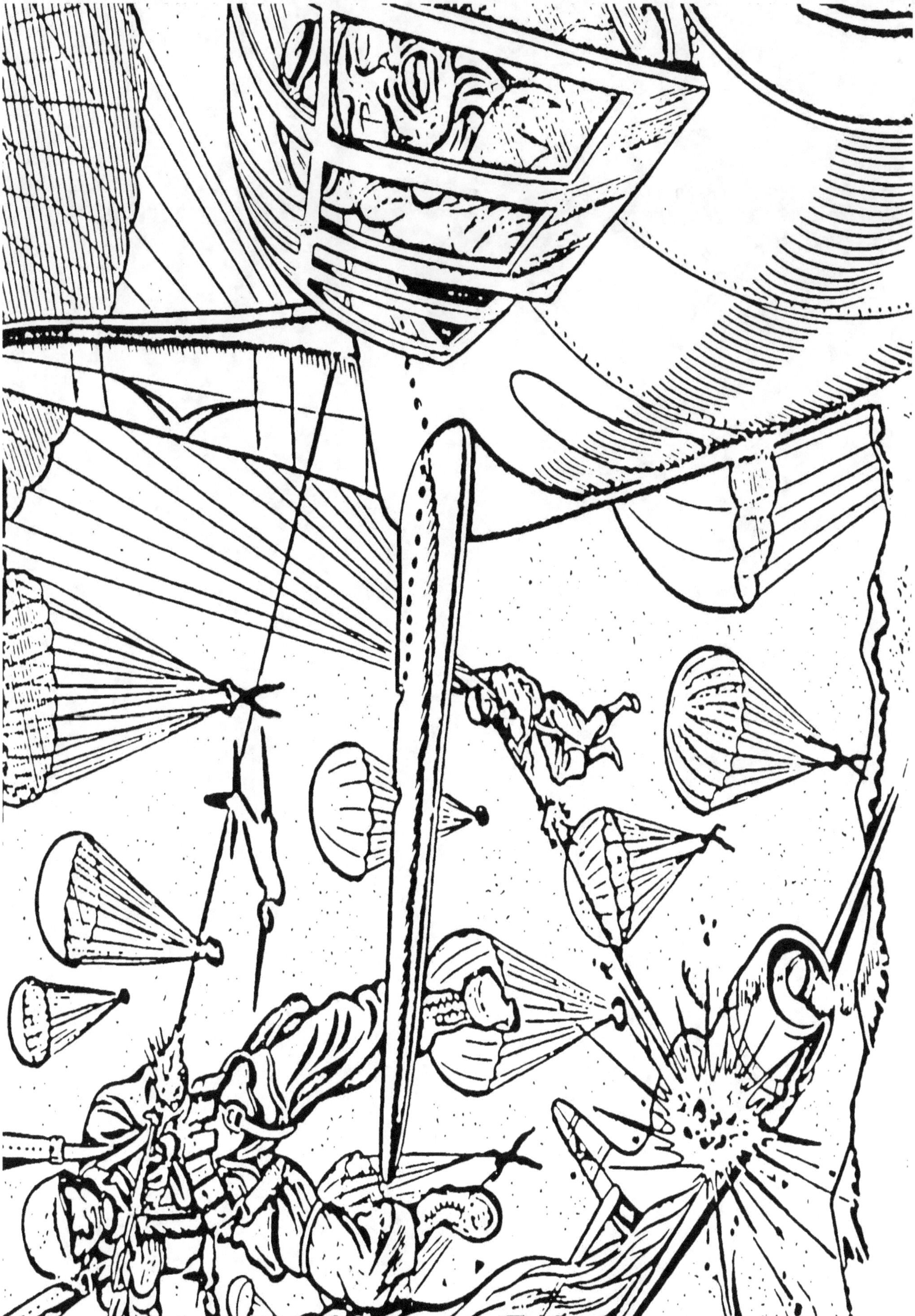

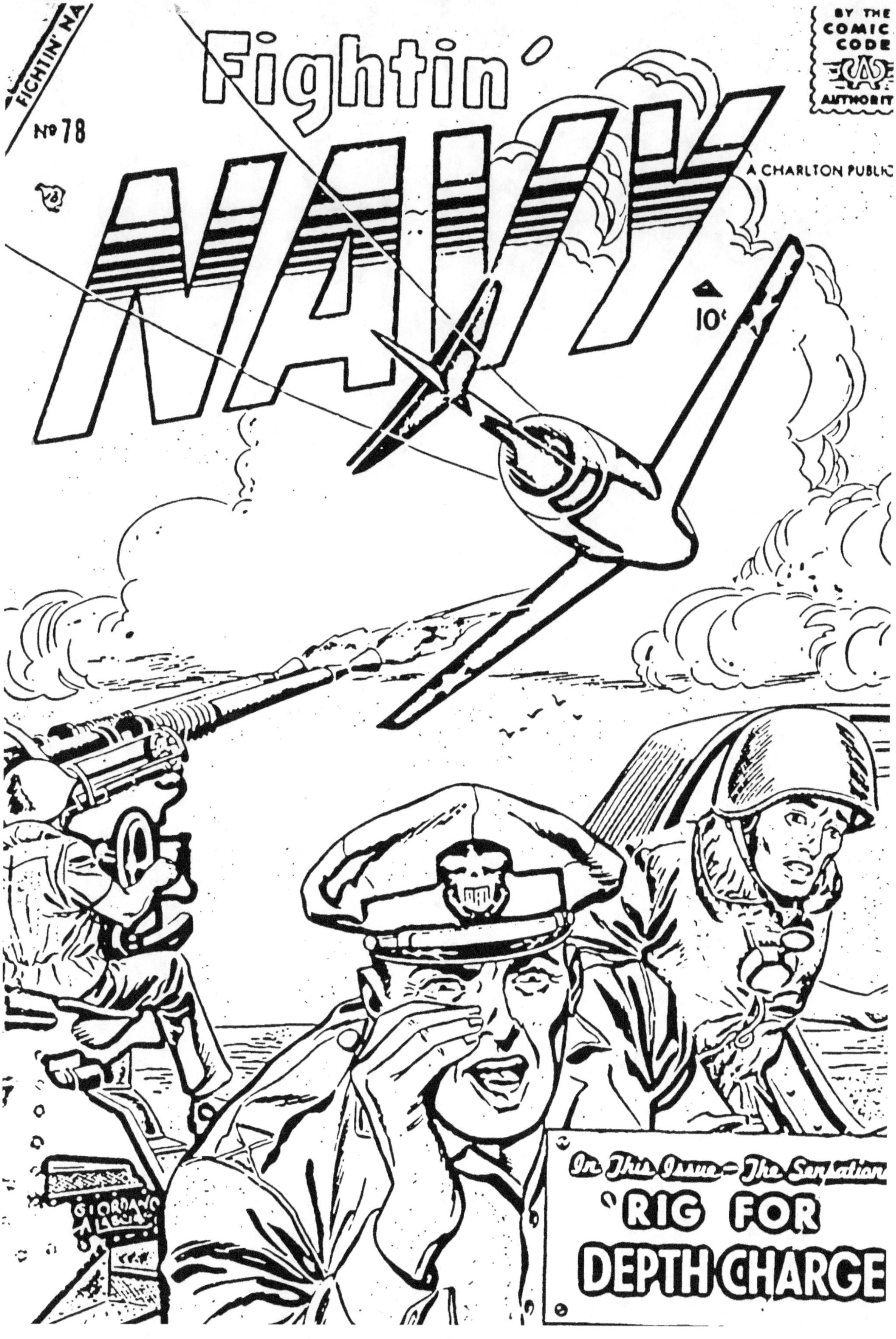
FIGHTIN' NA
No 78
Fightin'
NAVY
BY THE COMIC CODE AUTHORIT
A CHARLTON PUBLIC
10¢
In This Issue - The Sensation
'RIG FOR
DEPTH CHARGE

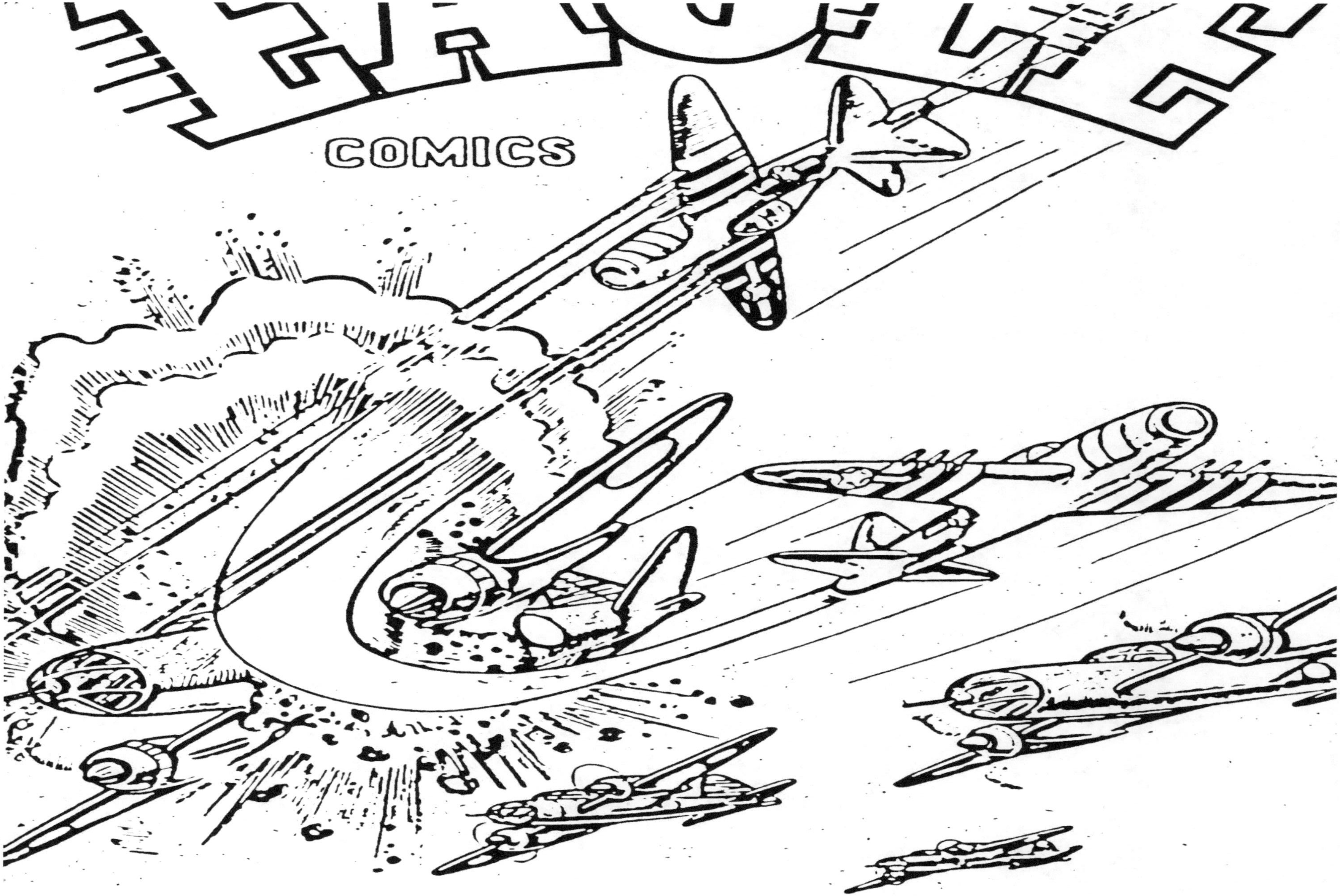
COMICS

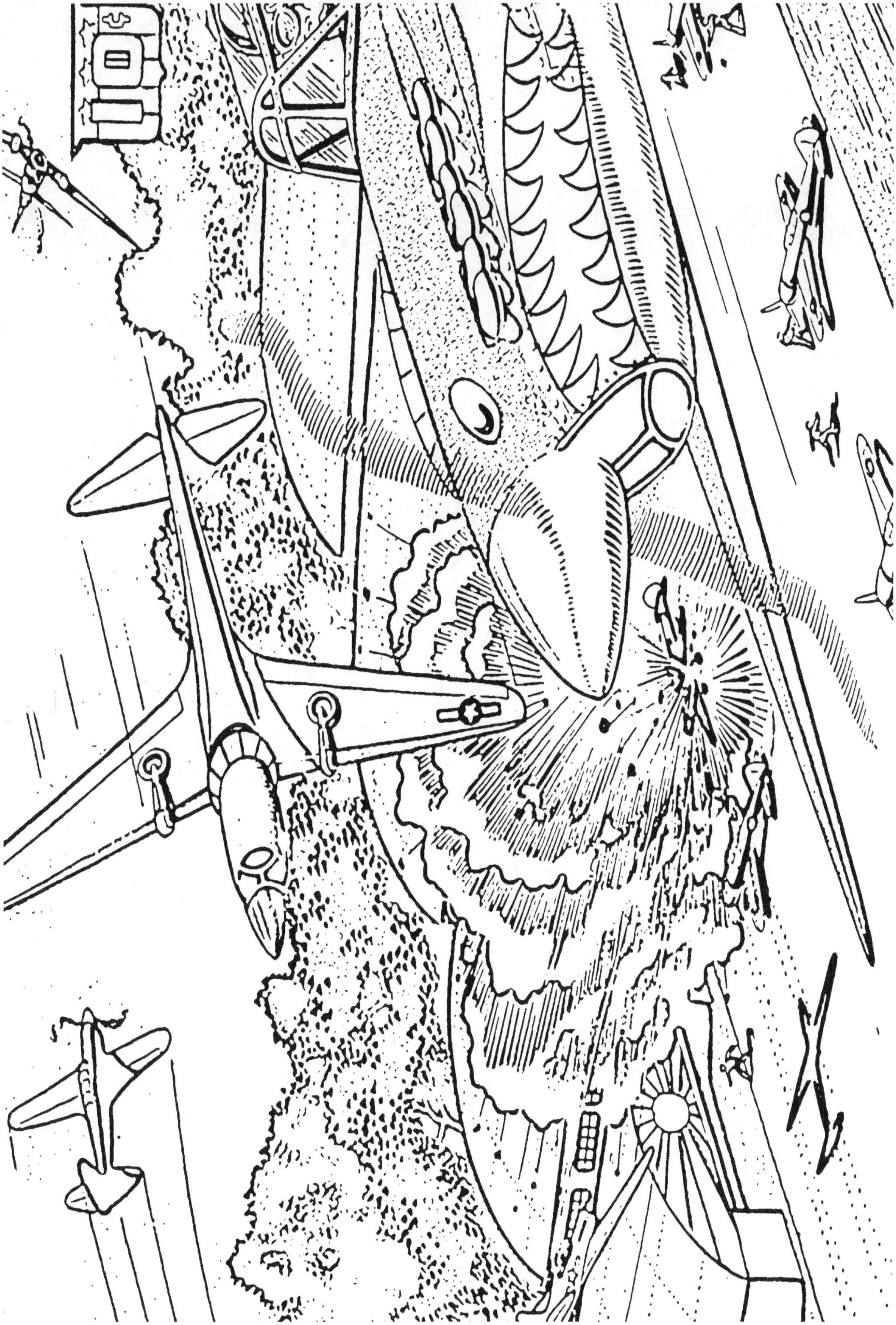

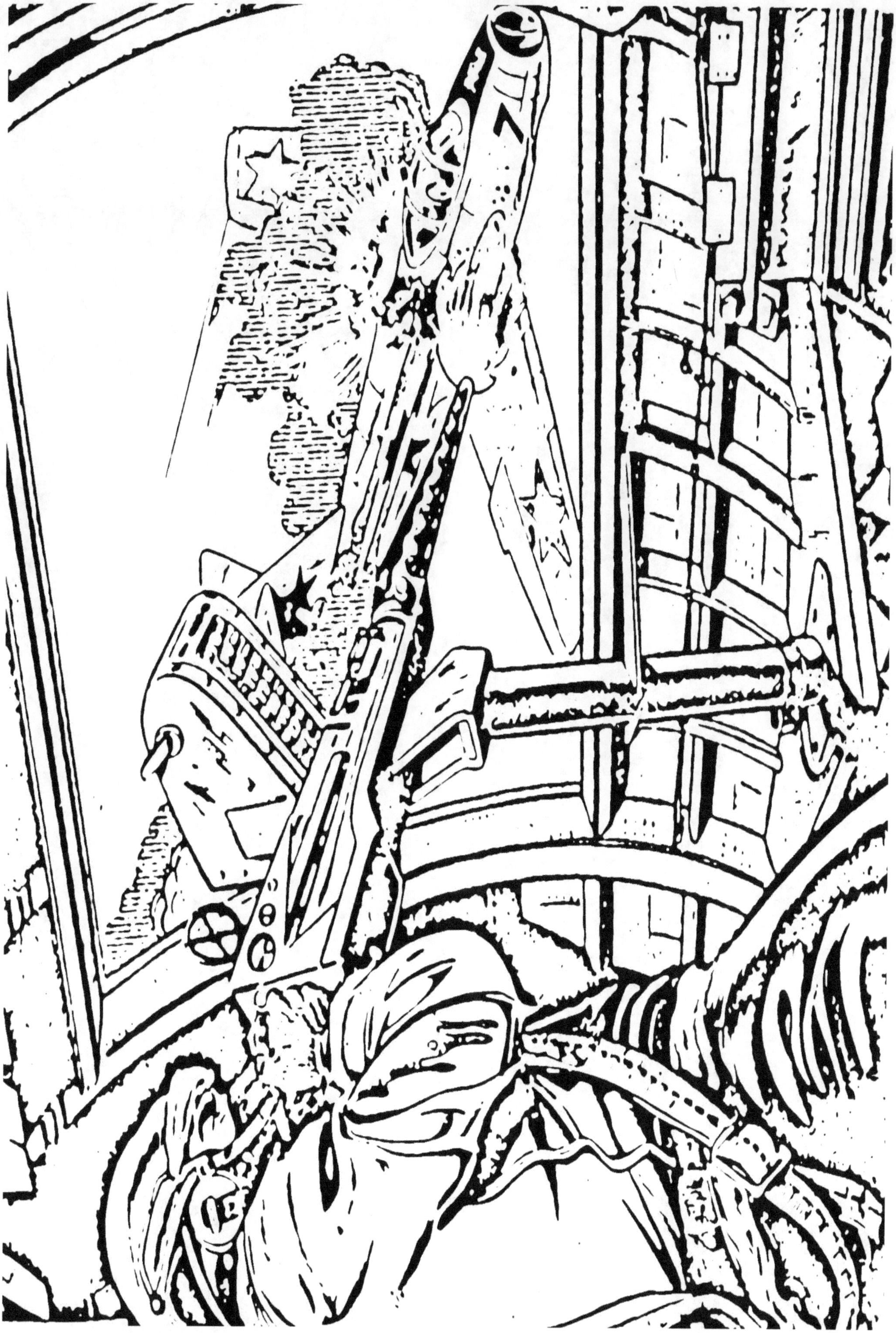

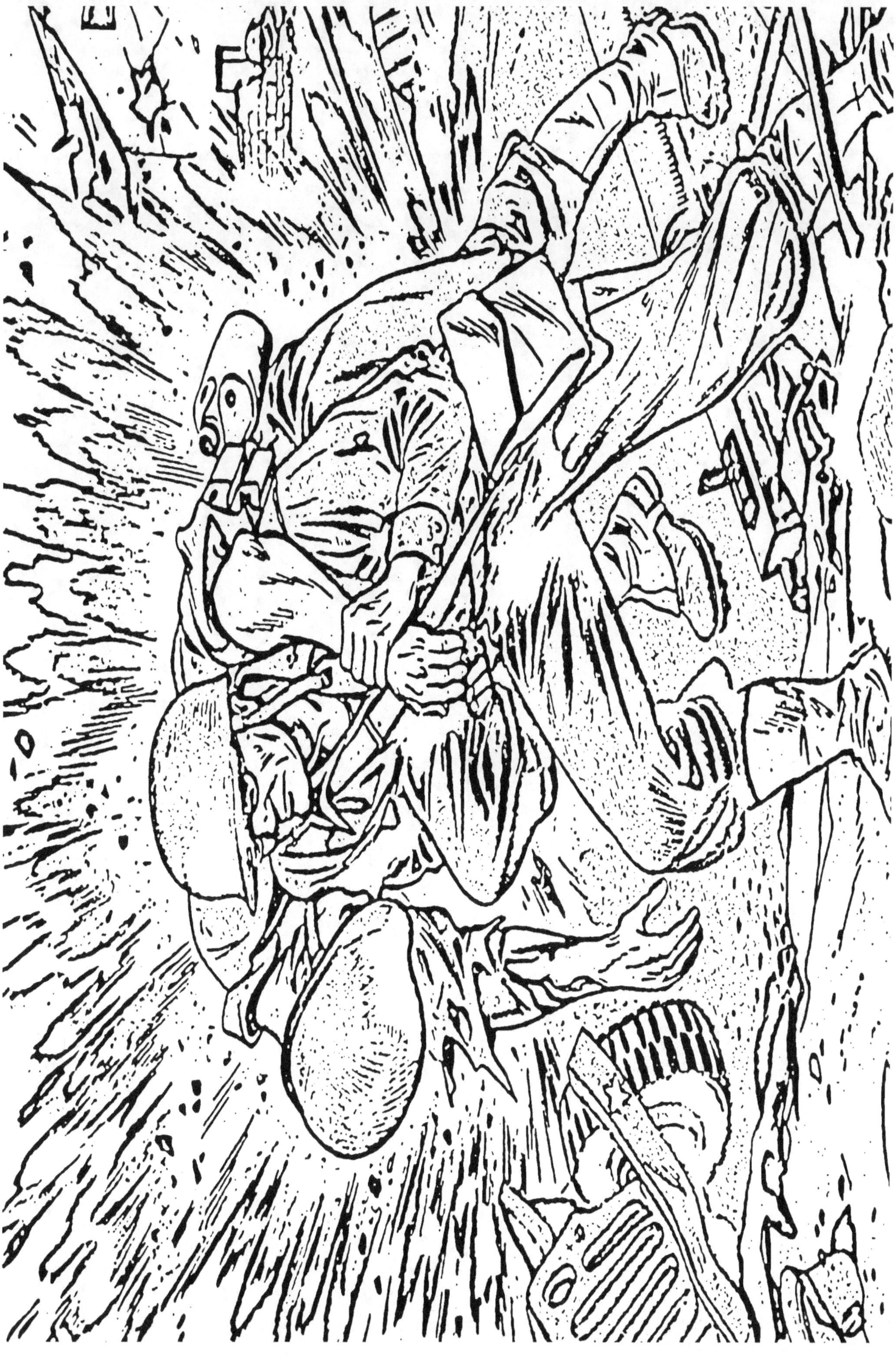

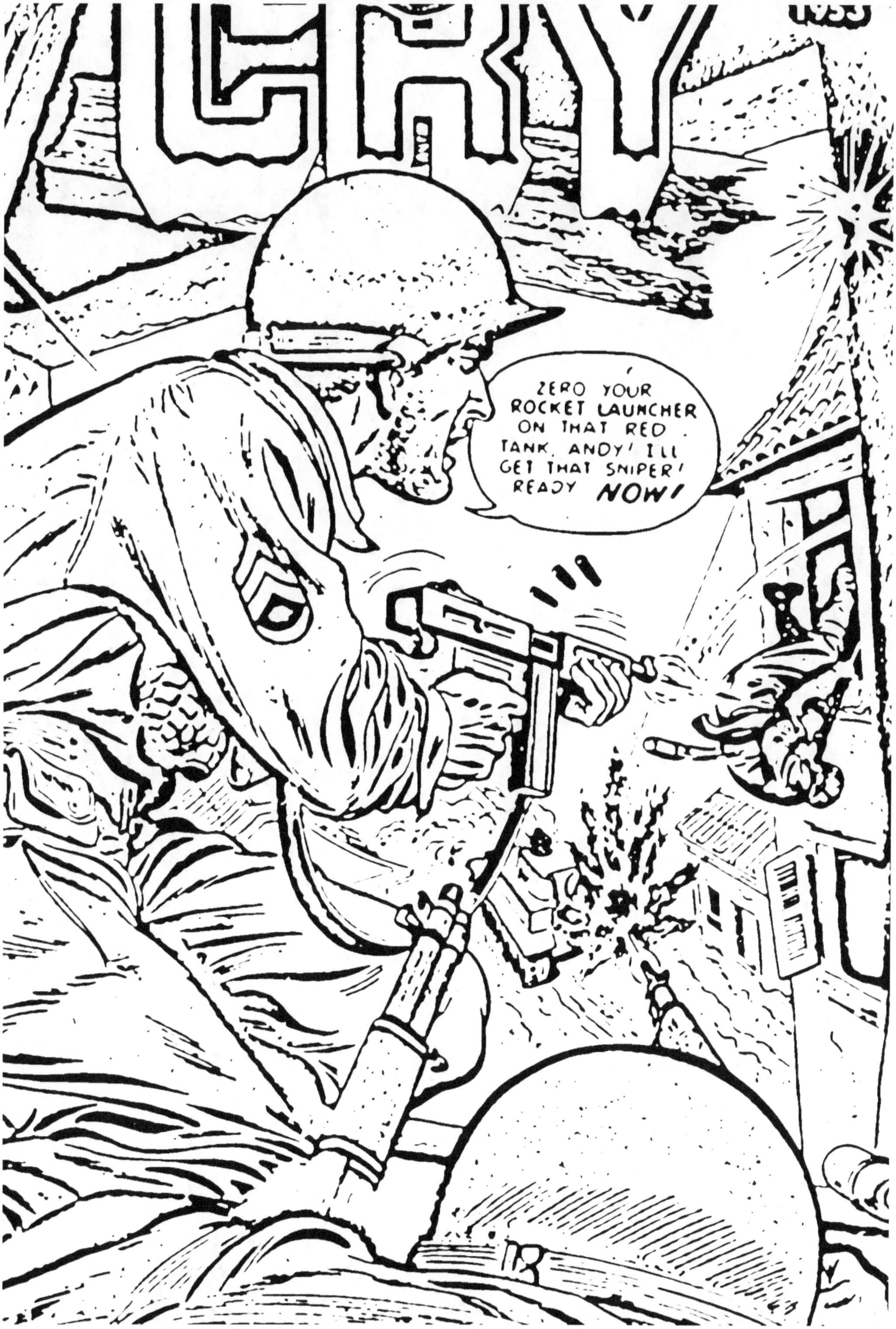
CRY
ZERO YOUR ROCKET LAUNCHER ON THAT RED TANK, ANDY! I'LL GET THAT SNIPER! READY NOW!

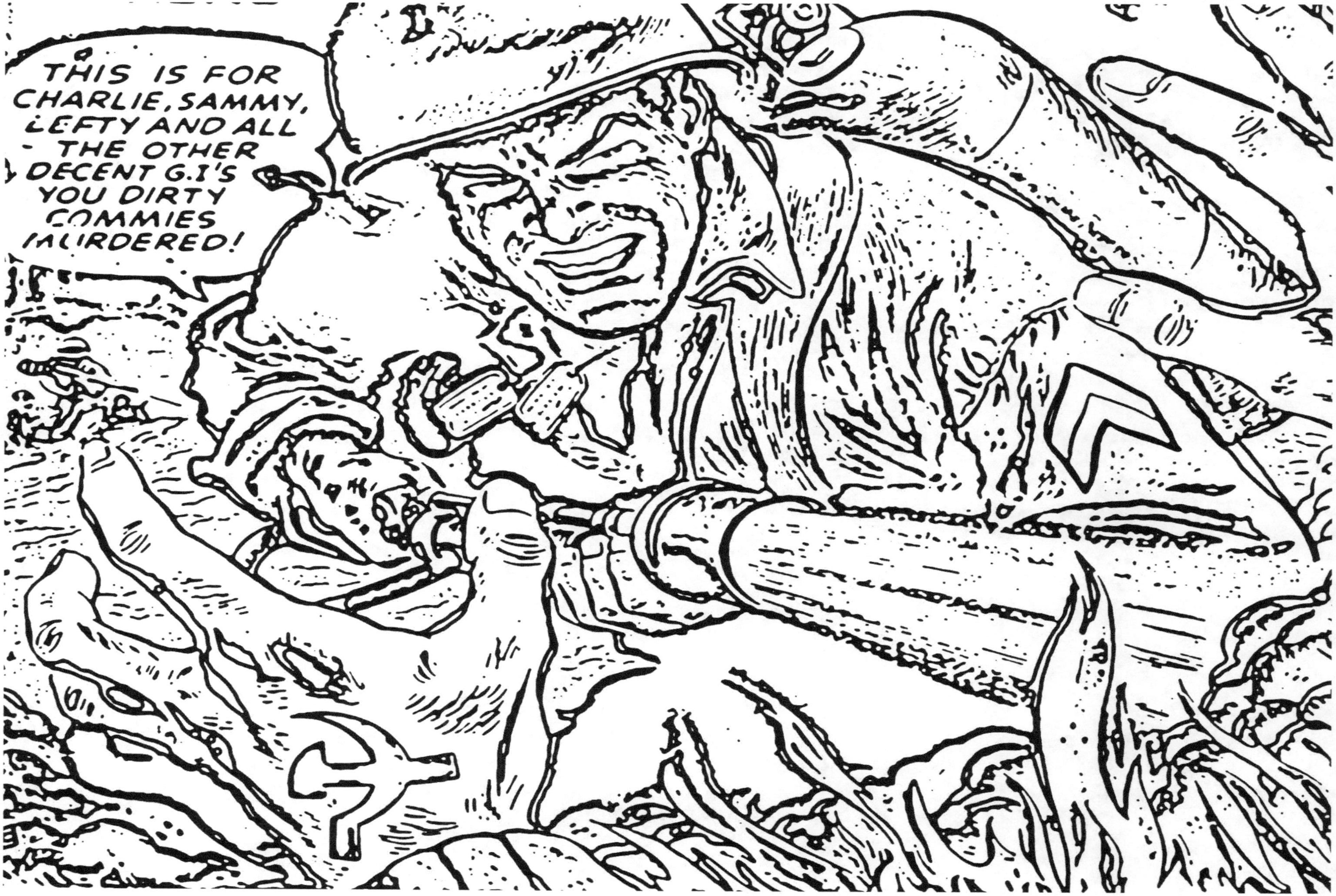
THIS IS FOR CHARLIE, SAMMY, LEFTY AND ALL THE OTHER DECENT G.I'S YOU DIRTY COMMIES MURDERED!

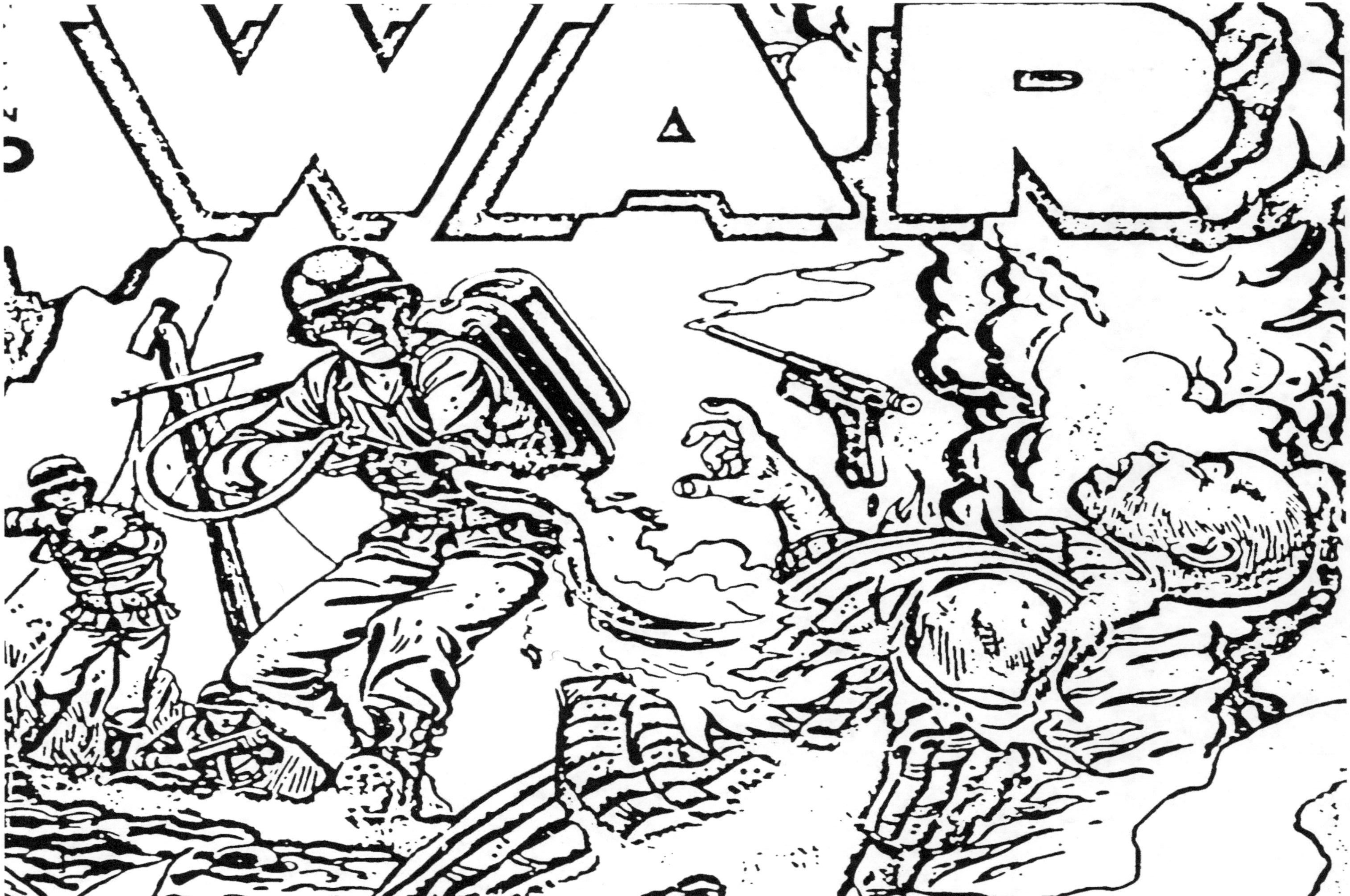
WAR

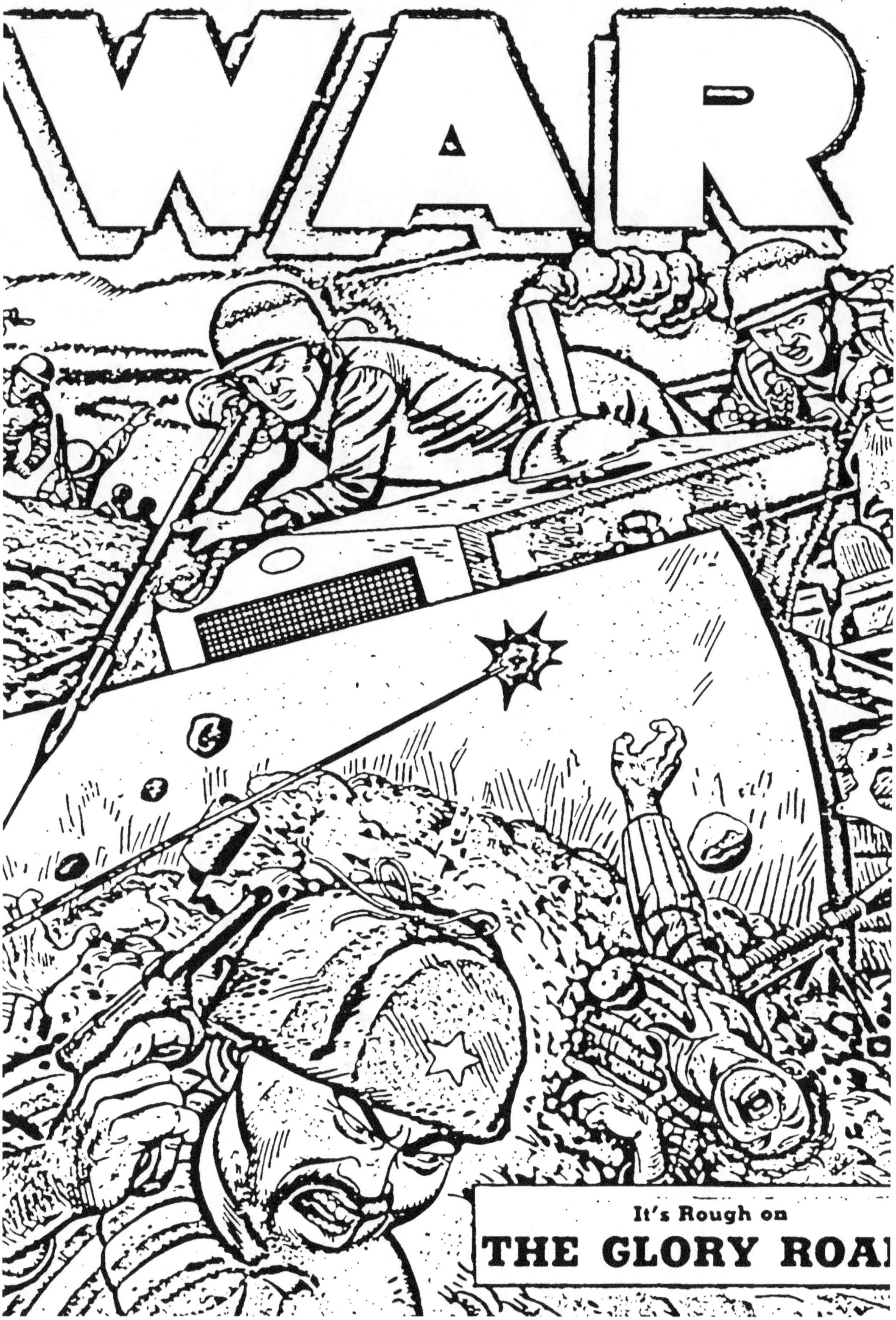
WAR
It's Rough on
THE GLORY ROA

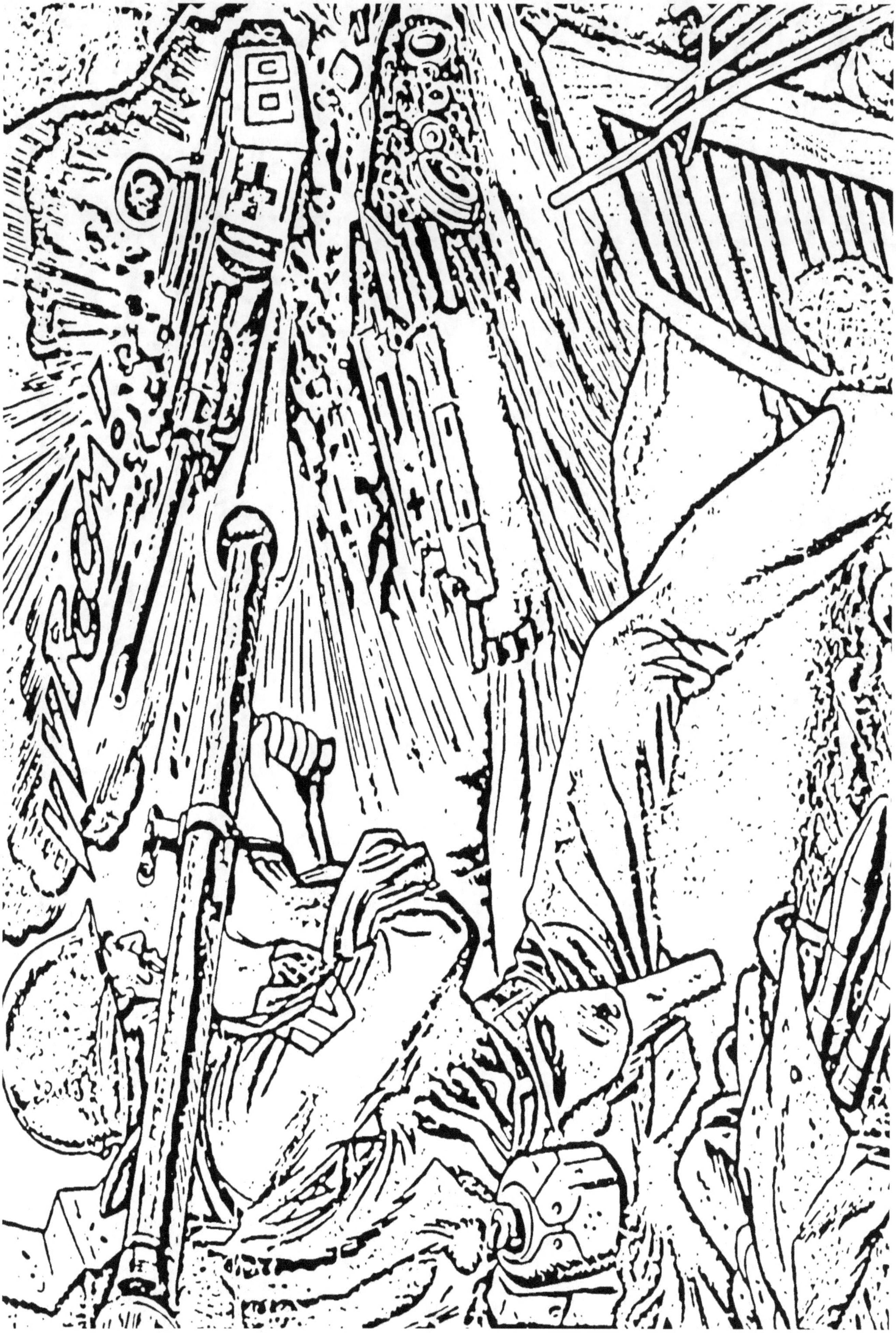

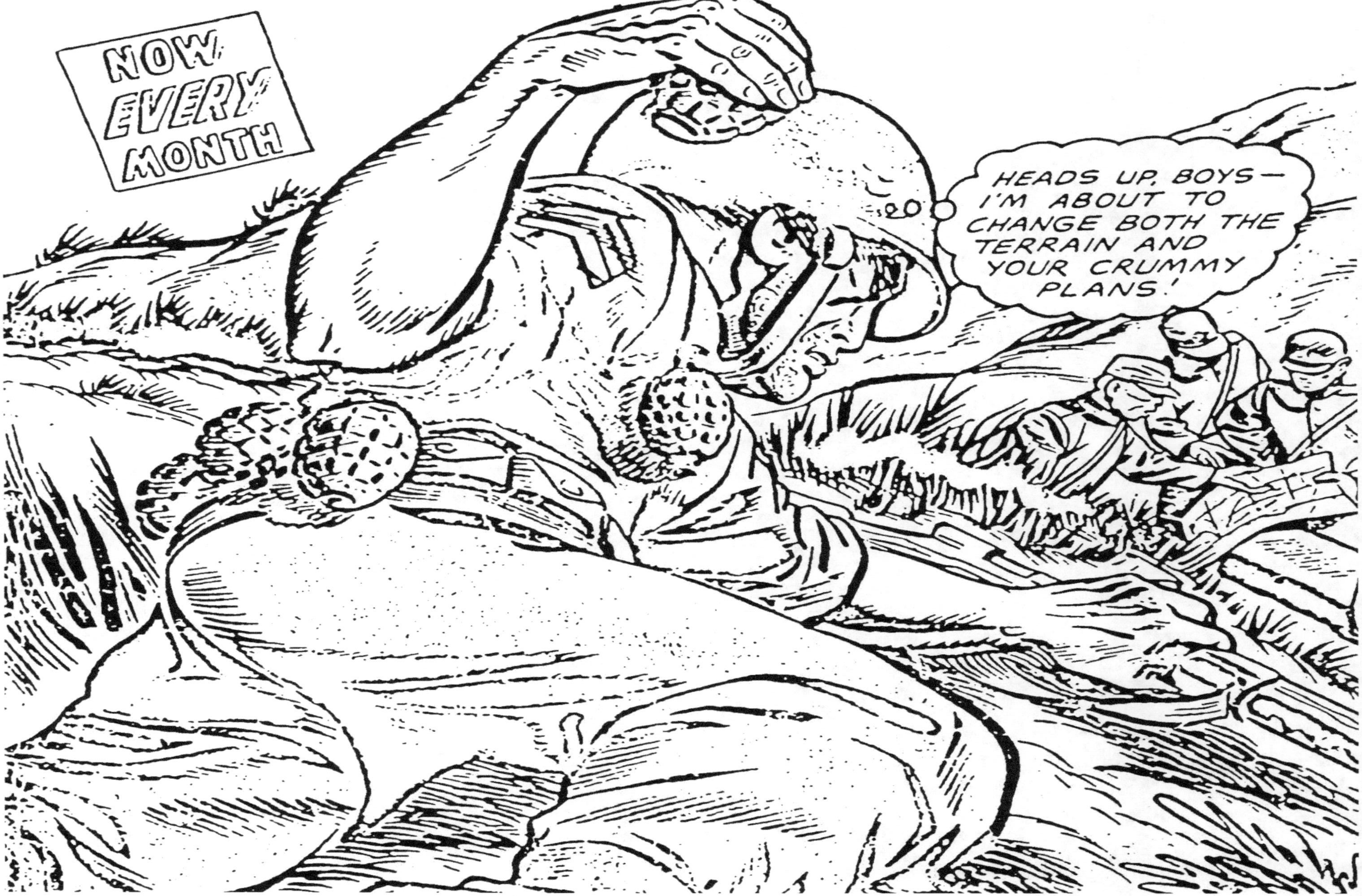
NOW EVERY MONTH
HEADS UP, BOYS— I'M ABOUT TO CHANGE BOTH THE TERRAIN AND YOUR CRUMMY PLANS!

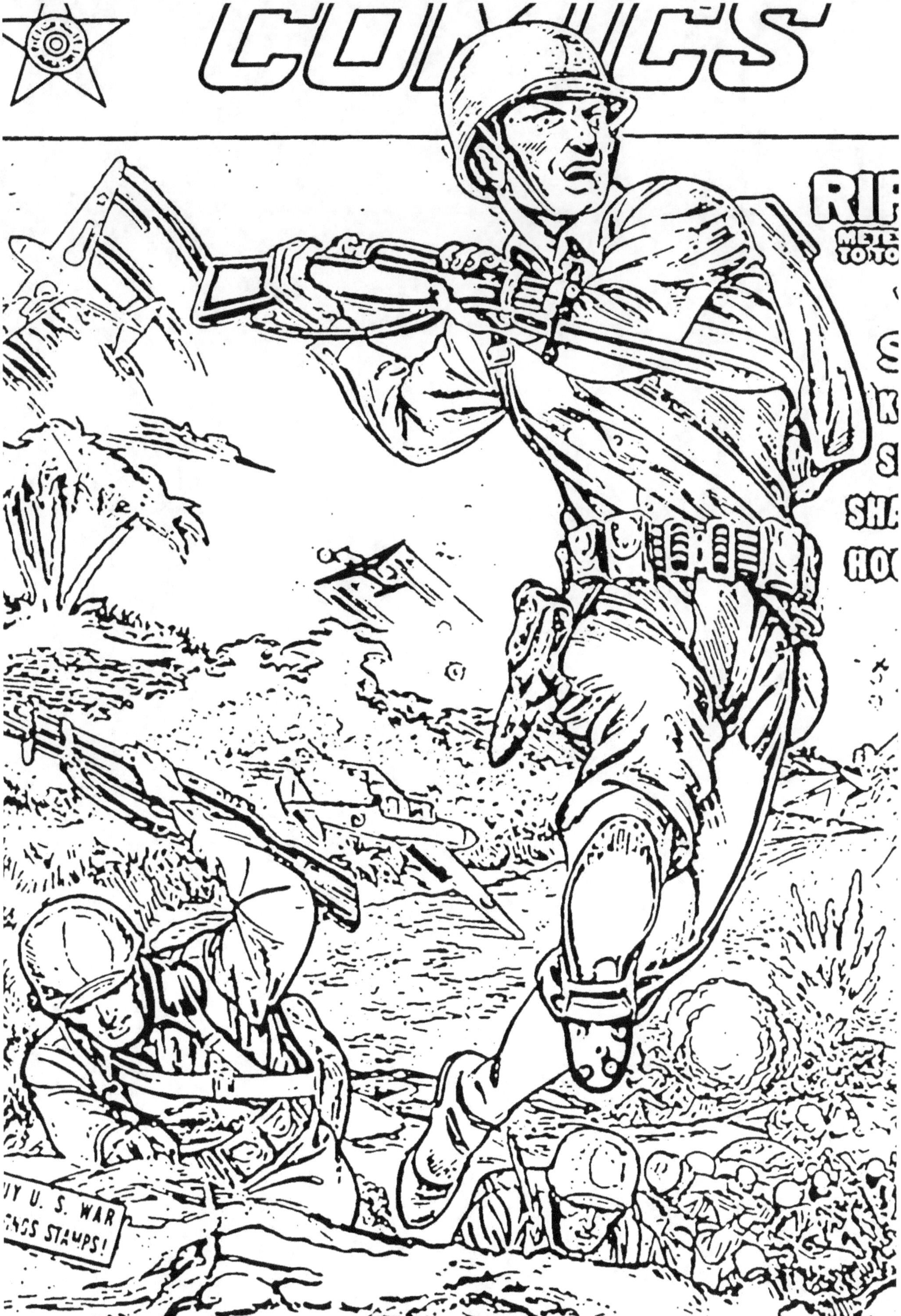
U. S. WAR
STAMPS!

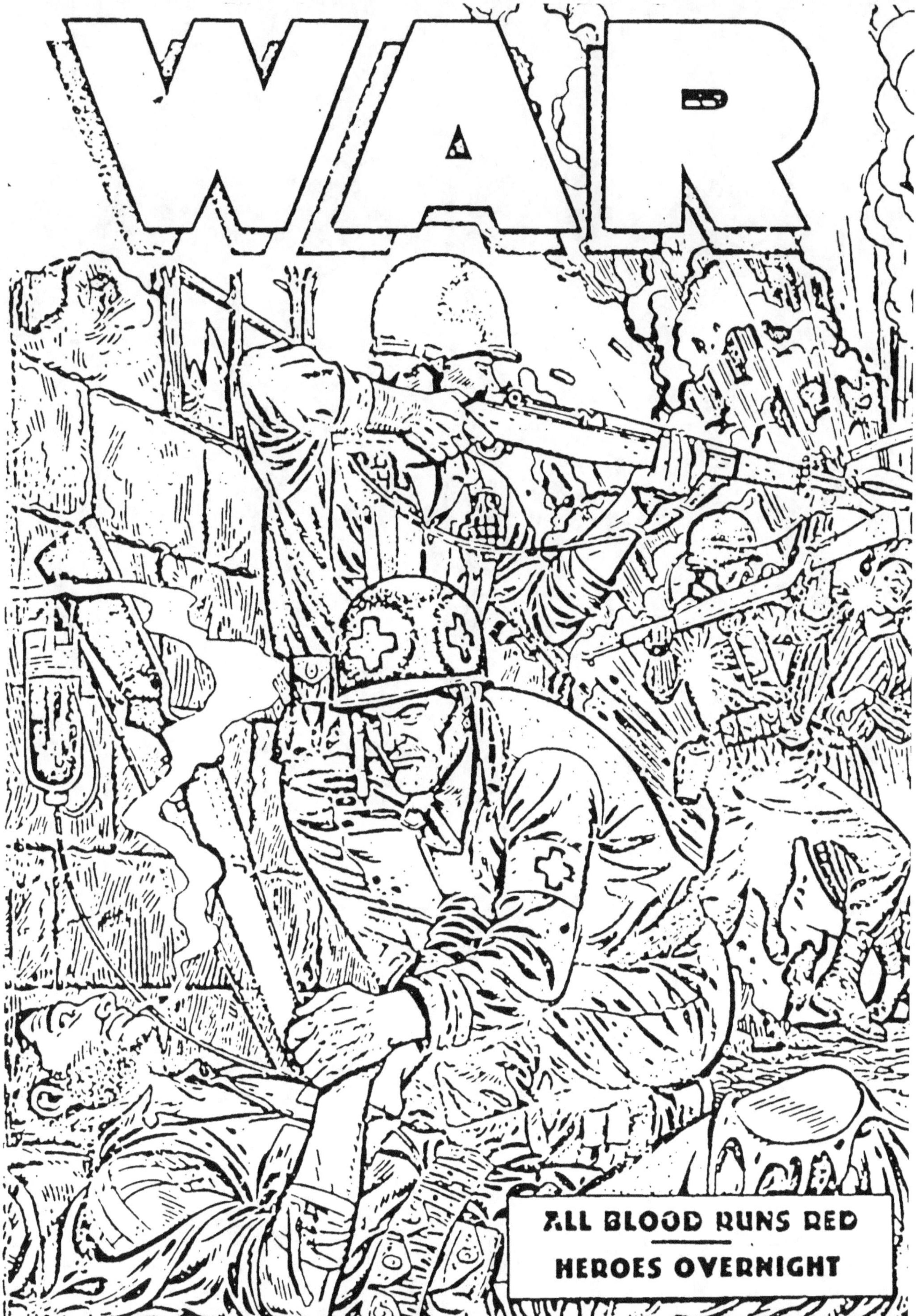
WAR
ALL BLOOD RUNS RED
HEROES OVERNIGHT

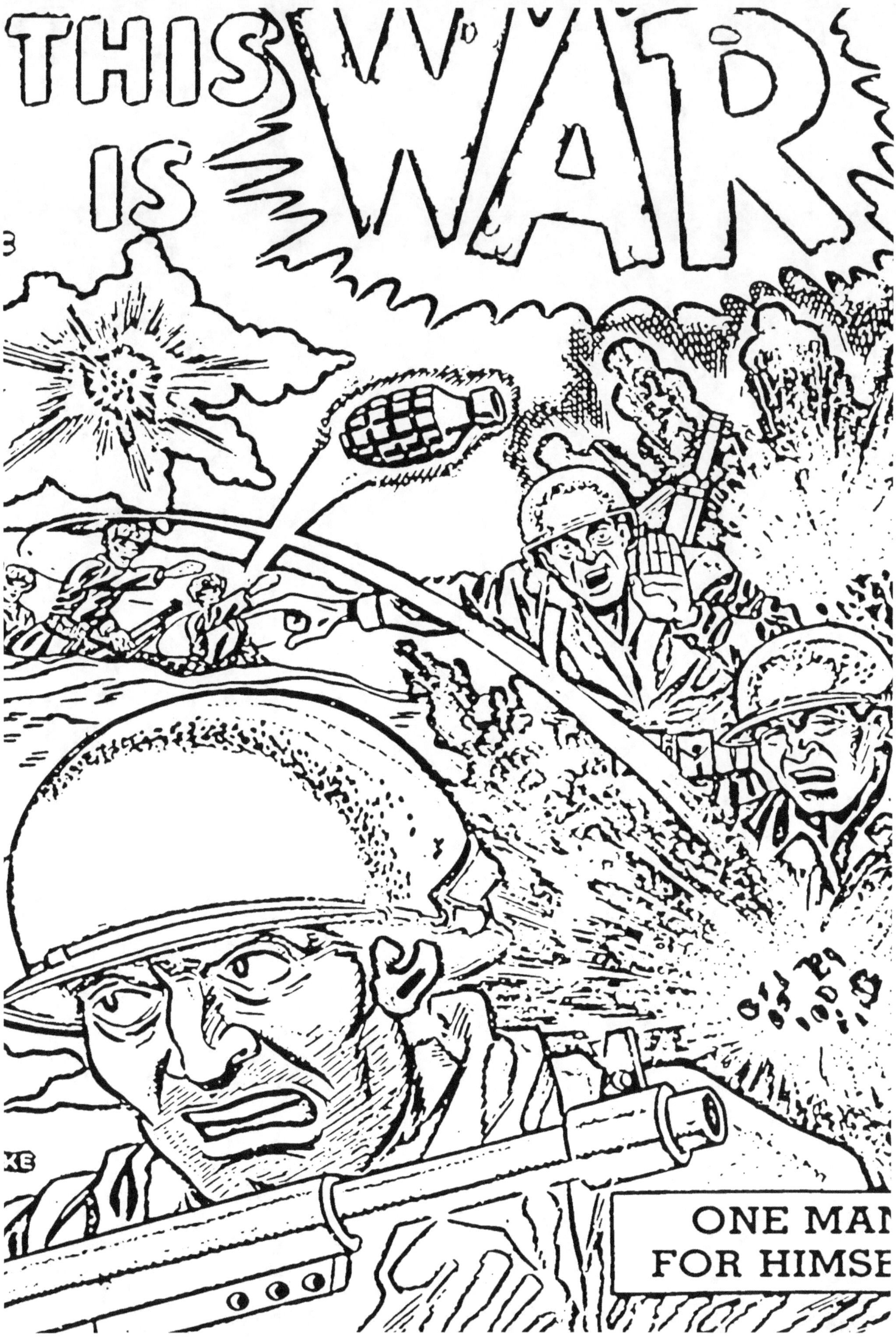
THIS IS WAR
ONE MA
FOR HIMSE

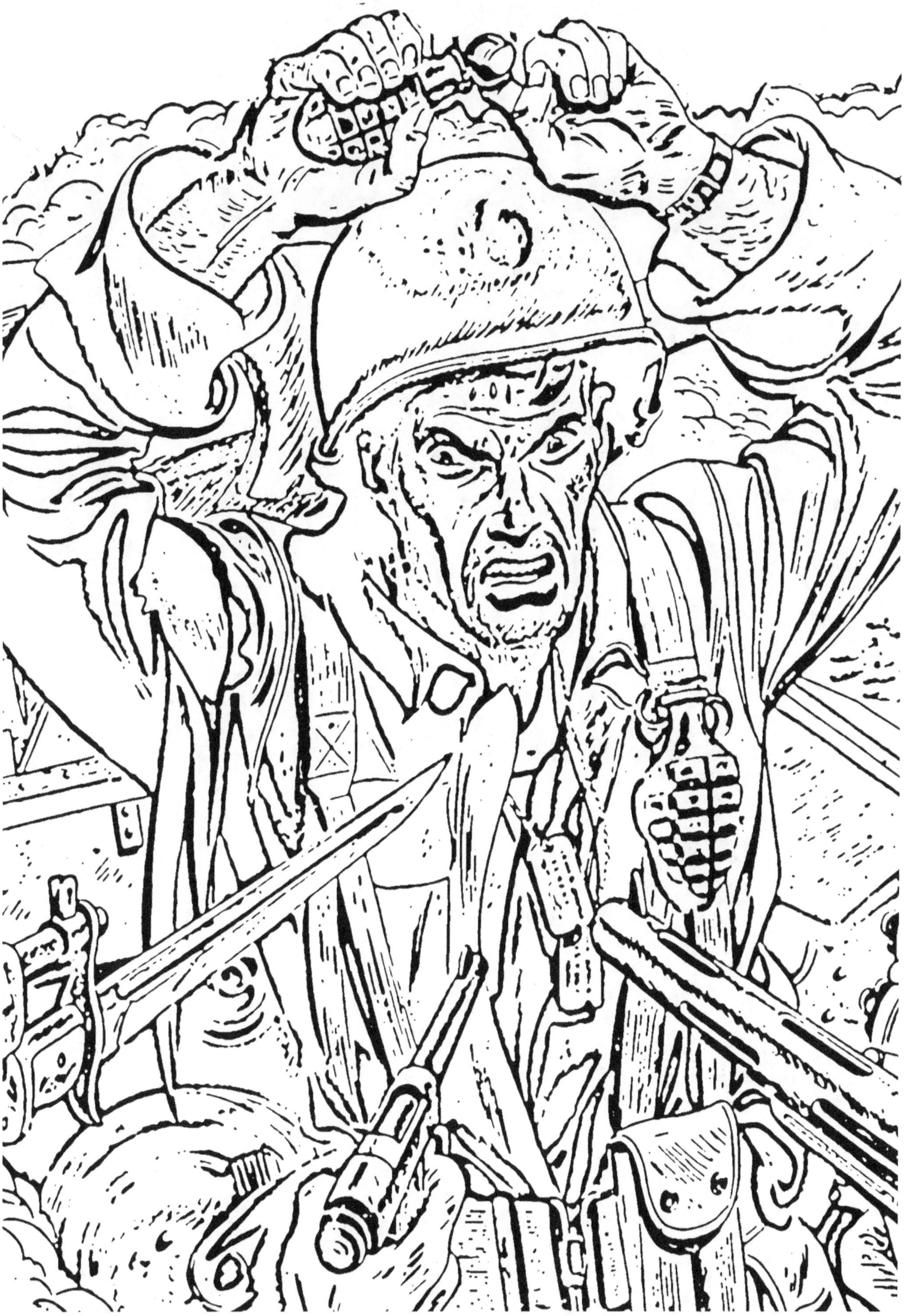

www.ingramcontent.com/pod-product-compliance
Lightning Source LLC
Chambersburg PA
CBHW080536190526
45169CB00007B/2525
9781534929401